Editorial Project Manager
Erica N. Russikoff, M.A.

Editor in Chief
Karen J. Goldfluss, M.S. Ed.

Creative Director
Sarah M. Fournier

Cover Artist
Sarah Kim

Illustrator
Mark Mason

Art Coordinator
Renée Mc Elwee

Imaging
Amanda R. Harter

Publisher
Mary D. Smith, M.S. Ed.

The Write

* Explores narrative, opinion/argumentative, and informative/explanatory writing
* Introduces diverse writing selections for modeling and analysis
* Targets essential paragraph features and critical essay components
* Encourages feedback through peer reviews, self-evaluations, and teacher input
* Lexile levels and standards correlations provided

OPINION
INFORMATIVE
NARRATIVE

Teacher Created Resources

Author
Tracie I. Heskett, M. Ed.

For correlations to the Common Core State Standards, see pages 157–160 of this book or visit *http://www.teachercreated.com/standards/*.

Cover photograph credits:
· Hot air balloon, ©Rick Willoughby (*https://www.flickr.com/photos/rickety/5053106800/*), CC BY 2.0.
· White tiger, ©Eric Kilby (*https://www.flickr.com/photos/ekilby/5611544753/*), CC BY-SA 2.0.
· Penny, ©Robert Couse-Baker (*https://www.flickr.com/photos/29233640@N07/6610387465/*), CC BY 2.0.
· Hand holding coins, ©TaxCredits.net (*https://www.flickr.com/photos/76657755@N04/7027595009/*), CC BY 2.0.

Teacher Created Resources
12621 Western Avenue
Garden Grove, CA 92841
www.teachercreated.com

ISBN: 978-1-4206-8011-9

© 2017 Teacher Created Resources
Made in U.S.A.

Teacher Created Resources

Table of Contents

Introduction

The Write Stuff is a series designed to help students build strong foundational skills in writing. To master the skills needed to write effectively, students benefit from guided instruction, analysis of writing models, and writing for a variety of audiences. The books in this series guide both teachers and students through the process of writing as it relates to three specific writing formats.

This book provides writing samples for students to study, as well as opportunities for students to write their own pieces. Students receive feedback on their writing in a variety of ways. They participate in peer reviews, complete self-evaluations, receive evaluations from the teacher, and compare differences in these assessments of their writing.

About This Book

Sections: The book is divided into three main sections, one for each type of writing students need to learn for college and career readiness: Opinion/Argumentative Writing, Informative/ Explanatory Writing, and Narrative Writing.

Themed Modules: Each section has two modules, or in-depth units.

First Module: This module presents a series of step-by-step lessons to introduce students to and teach the characteristics of that type of writing. Students read and discuss strong and weak examples of the type of writing in focus. Reading passages fall within the second-grade reading range based on Lexile estimates (420L–650L) for this grade level. Students then model what they learned to write a piece in that specific genre, from opening sentence to conclusion.

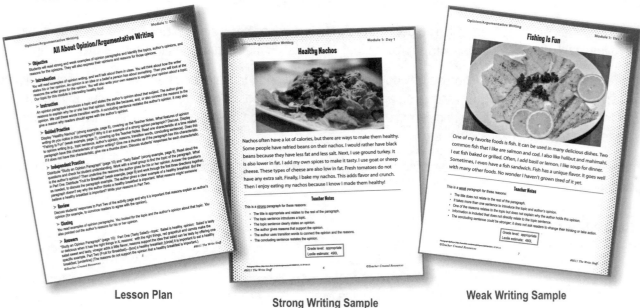

Lesson Plan   Strong Writing Sample   Weak Writing Sample

Second Module: This module provides additional experiences in which students learn about and practice writing a longer piece, or essay, in the focus genre. Each module suggests a topic for student writing. Additional related writing topics are listed at the back of the book on pages 155–156.

> Note: Modules 1, 3, and 5 require 10 days or class periods to complete, while Modules 2, 4, and 6 require seven days.

A chart on pages 157–160 lists the Common Core State Standards addressed in each lesson.

How to Use This Book

Each module includes writing samples written below, at, and above grade level as indicated. Lessons suggest how to incorporate the writing samples, although you may use them in other ways for additional practice. For example, conduct a shared-writing activity in which students work together as a class to mimic a sample paragraph about the same or a different topic. Alternatively, have students work with a partner to strengthen an example of a weak paragraph. Students may also work independently to practice writing paragraphs using one or more strong examples as a model.

When instructed, use a document camera or make photocopies onto transparencies (for overhead projectors) to display text. Cover the Teacher Notes with a piece of paper as needed during class discussion.

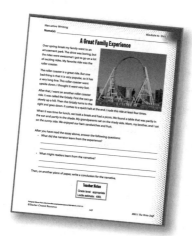

Each lesson begins with a scripted lesson plan. The script for the teacher is presented in italicized font. These lesson plans inform teachers about what to expect students to learn and be able to do. They enable teachers to make the best use of the time they have available for teaching writing in an already busy school day. The lessons include strategies that effectively help students learn to write.

Within each module, student activities build on one another. Answers to activities are provided on the lesson plan. Students focus on a single topic throughout the module as they work toward a finished product. You may wish to have students keep their activity pages in a folder for reference as they complete each lesson. Alternatively, you may refer to the related topics on pages 155–156 to give students additional writing experiences during lesson activities.

Guided Practice provides opportunities for students to work together as a whole class, in small groups, or with partners to focus on a particular aspect of the writing type in focus. Independent Practice offers additional activities for students to apply new skills as they write one or more parts of the work in progress.

Each module has one lesson in which students participate in a peer-review activity. Encourage students to offer positive feedback as well as constructive criticism that will motivate their classmates to improve their writing.

Students complete a self-evaluation activity during each module and then later compare the scores they assigned their own writing with scores they receive on a teacher evaluation. Rubrics provide objective statements about writing that help students analyze and reflect on their work with the goal of creating written selections that are more effective and engaging for readers.

Some activities ask students to research their topics. Refer to the following topic overview chart to plan and provide appropriate research resources.

➤ Topics Overview

Opinion/Argumentative	Module 1	Interesting Healthy Food
Opinion/Argumentative	Module 2	School Clothes
Informative/Explanatory	Module 3	Weather
Informative/Explanatory	Module 4	How Money Changes Over Time
Narrative	Module 5	Observing an Animal in Nature
Narrative	Module 6	Interesting Family Stories

All About Opinion/Argumentative Writing

➤ Objective

Students will read strong and weak examples of opinion paragraphs and identify the topics, author's opinions, and reasons for the opinions. They will also express their opinions and reasons for those opinions.

➤ Introduction

You will read examples of opinion writing, and we'll talk about them in class. You will think about how the writer states his or her opinion. An opinion is an idea or a belief a person has about something. Then you will look at the reasons the writer gives for the opinion. You will also write your own reasons to explain your opinion about a topic. Our topic for this module is interesting healthy food.

➤ Instruction

An opinion paragraph introduces a topic and states the author's opinion about that subject. The author gives reasons to explain why he or she has that opinion. Words like because, and, *or also* connect the reasons to the opinion. We call these words transition words. *A concluding sentence restates the author's opinion. It may also give a reason why readers should agree with the author's opinion.*

➤ Guided Practice

Display "Healthy Nachos" (strong example, page 6), covering up the Teacher Notes. *What features of opinion writing do you notice in this paragraph? Why is it an example of a strong opinion paragraph?* Discuss. Display "Fishing Is Fun" (weak example, page 7), covering up the Teacher Notes. Read one characteristic at a time related to opinion writing (e.g., topic sentence, author's opinion, reasons, transition words, concluding sentence). *Does this paragraph have this characteristic of opinion writing? Give me a thumbs up if the paragraph has this characteristic. If it does not have this characteristic, give me a thumbs down.* Discuss students' responses for each characteristic.

➤ Independent Practice

Distribute "Study an Opinion Paragraph" (page 10) and "Tasty Salad" (strong example, page 8). Read aloud the questions and check for student understanding. *Work with a small group to find the topic of the paragraph. What is the author's opinion? Then underline the reasons the author gives for his or her opinion. Answer the questions in Part One.* Distribute "Fruit for Breakfast" (weak example, page 9) and work through the first three directions together, as needed, to discuss the paragraph example. *The author gives a clear example of a healthy breakfast. But the paragraph doesn't say why the author thinks a healthy breakfast is important. What reasons might someone believe a healthy breakfast is important? Write your reasons in Part Two.*

➤ Review

Discuss students' responses to Part Two of the activity page and why it is important that reasons explain an author's opinion (for example, to convince readers to agree with the opinion).

➤ Closing

You read examples of opinion paragraphs. You looked for the topic and the author's opinion about that topic. You also pointed out the author's reasons for his or her opinion.

➤ Answers

"Study an Opinion Paragraph" (page 10): Part One (Tasty Salad)—*topic:* Salad is healthy. *opinion:* Salad is tasty or delicious when it has the right things in it; *reasons:* with the right things, red grapefruit and carrots make the salad sweet and tasty, vinegar adds a little flavor; reasons support the idea that salad can be tasty by offering one specific example. Part Two (Fruit for Breakfast)—[box] a healthy breakfast; [circle] It is important to eat a healthy breakfast; [underline] (The reasons do not support the opinion that a healthy breakfast is important.)

Healthy Nachos

Nachos often have a lot of calories, but there are ways to make them healthy. Some people have refried beans on their nachos. I would rather have black beans because they have less fat and less salt. Next, I use ground turkey. It is also lower in fat. I add my own spices to make it tasty. I use goat or sheep cheese. These types of cheese are also low in fat. Fresh tomatoes do not have any extra salt. Finally, I bake my nachos. This adds flavor and crunch. Then I enjoy eating my nachos because I know I made them healthy!

Teacher Notes

This is a <u>strong</u> paragraph for these reasons:

- The title is appropriate and relates to the rest of the paragraph.
- The topic sentence introduces a topic.
- The topic sentence clearly states an opinion.
- The author gives reasons that support the opinion.
- The author uses transition words to connect the opinion and the reasons.
- The concluding sentence restates the opinion.

Grade level: appropriate
Lexile estimate: 490L

Fishing Is Fun

One of my favorite foods is fish. It can be used in many delicious dishes. Two common fish that I like are salmon and cod. I also like halibut and mahimahi. I eat fish baked or grilled. Often, I add basil or lemon. I like soup for dinner. Sometimes, I even have a fish sandwich. Fish has a unique flavor. It goes well with many other foods. No wonder I haven't grown tired of it yet.

Teacher Notes

This is a <u>weak</u> paragraph for these reasons:

- The title does not relate to the rest of the paragraph.
- It takes more than one sentence to introduce the topic and author's opinion.
- One of the reasons relates to the topic but does not explain why the author holds this opinion.
- Information is included that does not directly relate to the topic sentence.
- The concluding sentence could be stronger; it does not ask readers to change their thinking or take action.

> Grade level: appropriate
> Lexile estimate: 480L

Name(s): _____

Tasty Salad

Salad is healthy and tasty. Some people think of salad as diet food. They might not think it tastes

good. But salad is delicious when it has the right things in it. One kind of salad I like has red cabbage

in it. I add red grapefruit and shredded carrots with the cabbage. These things make the salad a sweet,

tasty treat. I don't add a high-fat salad dressing. Instead, I use olive oil and vinegar. The vinegar adds a

little flavor, too. This kind of salad has vitamins and not very many calories. But it is a sweet, crunchy,

and delicious salad!

Teacher Notes

Grade level: appropriate
Lexile estimate: 520L

Fruit for Breakfast

It is important to eat a healthy breakfast. This helps you get ready for the whole day. Some people think oatmeal is bland. With the right ingredients, oatmeal is delicious. First, I don't use quick oats. I like to eat real oats, with milk. I ask a grown-up to cook the oats. Next, I add plenty of stuff to my oatmeal. But I don't add any sugar. I add cut up apples and raisins. Sometimes, I add blueberries and applesauce instead. For extra spice, I sprinkle cinnamon on top. All these things make my oatmeal taste great!

Teacher Notes

Grade level: below
Lexile estimate: 400L

Name(s): _____

Study an Opinion Paragraph

➤ Part One

Work with your group to find the topic of the paragraph "Tasty Salad" (page 8).

1. Write the topic in the box below.

    ```



    ```

2. Write what the author thinks about the topic in the oval below.

3. Underline the reasons the author lists for his or her opinion.

4. Do the reasons support the opinion? _____

5. How do you know? _____

    _____

6. After reading this paragraph, do you agree or disagree with the author? Why?

    _____

    _____

➤ Part Two: Fruit for Breakfast

Read "Fruit for Breakfast" (page 9). Then follow the directions below.

1. Draw a box around the topic of the paragraph.

2. Circle the author's opinion.

3. Underline the reasons the author lists for his or her opinion, if any.

4. What other reasons can you think of to explain why the author has this opinion? Write your ideas below.

    _____

    _____

    _____

    _____

    _____

Topic Sentences

➤ Objective

Students will participate in a listening activity and class discussion, then read and identify topic sentences on their own. They will brainstorm possible topics for their opinion paragraphs and write topic sentences.

➤ Introduction

You will listen to sentences as I read them aloud. Then you will talk about what makes a sentence a good topic sentence for an opinion paragraph. You will also read topic sentences on your own. Then you will brainstorm topics for your opinion paragraph. You will use your ideas to write a topic sentence for your opinion paragraph.

➤ Instruction

The topic sentence for an opinion paragraph introduces the subject. It tells what the paragraph will be about. A strong topic sentence says what the author thinks or believes about the topic. This is the author's opinion. An opinion is an idea someone has about something. It is what someone thinks or feels about a topic.

➤ Guided Practice

Distribute an index card to each student. *Write the words* topic sentence *on the card I gave you.* Display sample paragraphs on the whiteboard or chart paper, for example, from a classroom book about healthy food. *Which sentence is the topic sentence? Listen as I read each sentence in the paragraph. When I read a sentence that tells what the paragraph will be about, raise your topic sentence card. If I read a sentence that says the author's opinion, raise your topic sentence card.* Discuss the features of sentences that students identify as topic sentences.

➤ Independent Practice

Distribute "Strong Topic Sentences" (page 12). *A strong topic sentence has two parts: a topic and an opinion. Read each sentence. Draw a wavy line beside the sentence if it introduces a topic. Ask yourself, "Do I know what this paragraph will be about?" Draw a star beside the sentence if it tells the author's opinion. Ask yourself, "Do I know what the author thinks or believes about this topic?"*

Distribute "Writing a Topic Sentence" (page 13). *Writers use certain words that let readers know a sentence tells the author's opinion. Circle the words in the sentence stems in Part One that show the sentence will give an opinion. In Part Two, you will brainstorm healthy and interesting foods you like to eat. Then answer the questions to think about why you like these foods. Choose one food and reason and write a topic sentence for your healthy food paragraph.*

➤ Review

Clarify that a strong topic sentence introduces the topic (what the paragraph will be about) as well as the author's opinion about that topic (what the author thinks or believes about the topic).

➤ Closing

You learned what makes a strong topic sentence. You also brainstormed your ideas for an opinion paragraph and practiced writing a topic sentence.

➤ Answers

"Strong Topic Sentences" (page 12): 1. wavy line, star; 2. star; 3. topic and opinion are unclear; 4. star; 5. wavy line, star; 6. wavy line, star; 7. wavy line; 8. topic and opinion are too broad.

"Writing a Topic Sentence" (page 13): Part One—1. like; 2. believe; 3. think; 4. best

Name(s): _____

Strong Topic Sentences

A strong topic sentence has two parts, a *topic* and an *opinion*.

Read each sentence. Draw a wavy line ～～～ beside the sentence if it introduces a topic. Ask yourself, "Do I know what this paragraph will be about?"

Draw a star ☆ beside the sentence if it tells the author's opinion. Ask yourself, "Do I know what the author thinks or believes about this topic?"

Note: Not all sentences will need a symbol.

1. I like to eat tomatoes because they are healthy.

2. My favorite healthy food is grilled salmon.

3. More people are eating healthy foods now.

4. In the summer, I like to have juicy peaches for a healthy breakfast.

5. I would like to try a new healthy food like dragon fruit.

6. Apples are a healthy food that is easy to eat.

7. Kids can choose healthy foods to eat.

8. There are many different kinds of healthy foods.

Photograph ©Katrin Gilger (*https://www.flickr.com/photos/diekatrin/4363072620/*), CC BY-SA 2.0.

Writing a Topic Sentence

➤ Part One

An *opinion* is an idea someone has about something. It is what someone thinks or feels about a topic.

Writers use certain words that let readers know a sentence tells the author's opinion. Circle the words in the sentence stems below that show the author is giving an opinion.

1. I like this food because . . .

2. I believe this food is healthy because . . .

3. I think people should eat this healthy food because . . .

4. The best healthy food for kids to eat is . . .

➤ Part Two

Write the names of interesting healthy foods you like to eat in the box below. Answer the questions below for one or more of the foods you listed.

1. Why do I like this food? _____
   _____

2. Why do I believe this food is healthy? _____
   _____

3. Why do I think people should eat this healthy food? _____
   _____

4. Why is this the best healthy food for kids to eat? _____
   _____

Choose one sentence you wrote above as the topic sentence for your paragraph. What will your paragraph be about? What do you want to say about this food? Write your sentence below.

_____

_____

_____

Supporting Details

➤ Objective
Students will brainstorm descriptive words and then complete graphic organizers specific to their topics. They will also read a sample paragraph to identify reasons for an author's opinion and consider which reasons apply to their topics. Students will draw on ideas generated in this lesson to write reasons for their opinions.

➤ Introduction
What are the five senses? You will think about them to brainstorm descriptive words with the class and with a small group. Then you will read a sample paragraph. You will find the reasons the author gives for his or her opinion. You will think about how these reasons might connect to the topic. Then you will write your own reasons to explain your opinion in your paragraph.

➤ Instruction
An opinion paragraph has details and examples. Details are words that describe something exactly. They tell why the writer thinks or feels a certain way about the topic. These details give reasons that explain the author's opinion. Sensory words give writers a way to describe the topic and say why they have this opinion. You will write reasons for your opinion. Ask yourself why you think the food is interesting or healthy. Answer your "why" question with descriptive words that add details to your reason.

➤ Guided Practice
As a class, brainstorm sensory descriptive words. *What are some words that describe the way different foods look, smell, taste, feel, and sound when you eat them?* Write students' contributions on the whiteboard or chart paper for student reference. Arrange students in small groups and distribute "Descriptive Words" (page 15). *Take turns sharing your topic for your opinion paragraph with your group. Help each other brainstorm words that describe each food using the five senses. Look at our class notes for ideas.* Encourage students to use resources, such as beginning dictionaries, to clarify and understand word nuances and meanings.

➤ Independent Practice
Distribute "Reasons for My Opinion" (page 16) and "Healthy Nachos" (page 6). *Work with your partner to complete the chart in Part One. Reread the sample paragraph. List the reasons the author gives that explain how or why this food is healthy or interesting.*

Write a check mark to show whether each reason tells why the food is healthy or interesting or both. In the last column, write yes or no if the reason might apply to your topic. Brainstorm with your partner. Why might someone find this food healthy or interesting? Write your reasons in the blank lines on the chart and check the columns for your new reasons. Then work with your partner to complete Part Two. Think about the descriptive words you have brainstormed in this lesson to complete the sentences.

➤ Review
Use the sentence stems on "Reasons for My Opinion" to model how to write a reason, as necessary.

➤ Closing
You have worked together with classmates to think of descriptive words. You also listed a writer's reasons from a sample paragraph. You used these ideas to write reasons for your opinion in your opinion paragraph.

➤ Answers
"Reasons for My Opinion" (page 16): *reasons*—Black beans have less fat (H); Black beans have less salt (H); Ground turkey is lower in fat (H); Spices make it tasty (I); Goat or sheep cheese is low in fat (H, I); Fresh tomatoes do not have extra salt (H, I); Baking the nachos adds flavor and crunch (I).

Name(s): _____

Descriptive Words

- Write your topic in the center circle.

- Work with your group to think of sensory words that describe your interesting healthy food.

- Write your ideas in the circles below.

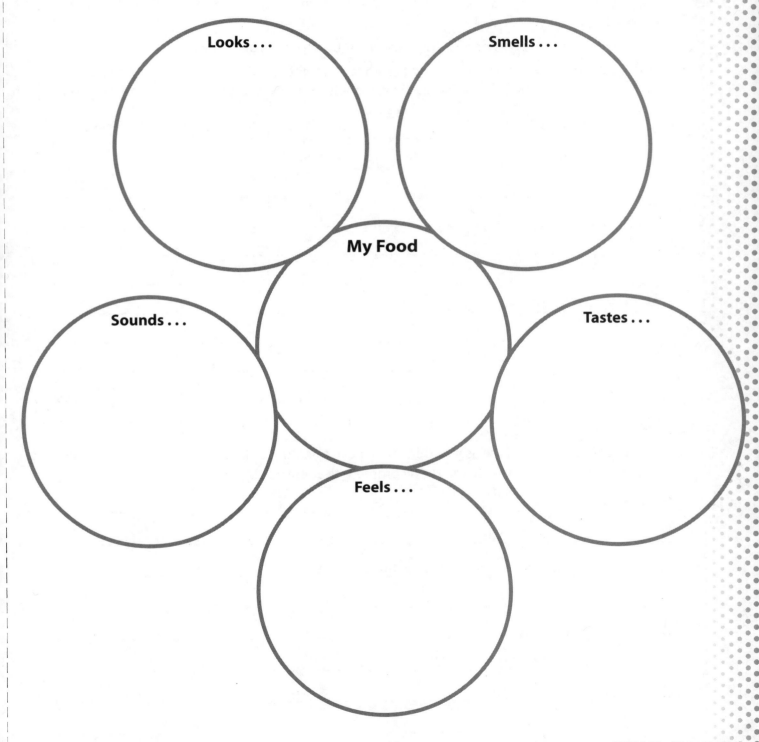

Name(s): _____

Reasons for My Opinion

➤ Part One

1. Reread "Healthy Nachos" (page 6).

2. In the first column, write the food and reasons the author gives that explain how or why this food is healthy or interesting.

3. In the next two columns, make a check mark to show if each reason tells why the food is healthy or interesting or both.

4. In the last column, write *yes* or *no* if the reason might apply to your topic.

5. Brainstorm with your partner other reasons someone might find this food healthy or interesting. Write your reasons in the blank lines on the chart and check the columns for your new reasons.

Food and Reason	Healthy	Interesting	My Food

➤ Part Two

Discuss with your partner the reasons you think this food is healthy or interesting. Think about the words you wrote in the previous activity. Then complete the sentences.

1. I think my food is _____ because _____

    _____.

2. One reason other people might want to eat this food is _____

    _____.

3. My food is healthy because _____

    _____.

4. My food is interesting because _____

    _____.

Transition Words

➤ Objective

Students will observe a model of how to write sentences using transition words to connect reasons with an opinion and with other reasons. Then they will identify transition words in sample sentences, think about the reasons for their opinions, and practice writing sentences with transition words.

➤ Introduction

You will see examples of sentences with transition words. Then you will find the transition words in sentences on your own. You will also think about the opinion you have about your topic and your reasons for that opinion. You will practice writing your own sentences with transition words.

➤ Instruction

Authors use certain words to connect their reasons with their opinions. We call these words transition words. *A word such as* because *tells why the author has his or her opinion about the topic. Authors use words like* and *or* also *to give more than one reason for an opinion. These words help authors connect reasons together. Other words that authors use to connect ideas and reasons are* but, if, since, so, *and* then.

➤ Guided Practice

Think aloud and model writing reasons and transition words to connect the reasons to an opinion. For example, rewrite and display reasons from "Fishing Is Fun" (page 7). *What is the author's opinion about this topic?* (Fish is one of the author's favorite foods; it is delicious.) *What are the author's reasons for this opinion?* (Fish has a unique flavor. It goes well with other foods. The author eats it baked or grilled.) *How could transition words be added to connect each reason to the opinion or to another reason?* (One of my favorite foods is fish *because* it is delicious. Fish has a unique taste. It *also* goes well with other foods. I like to eat it grilled *and* I add lemon for extra flavor.)

➤ Independent Practice

Distribute "Connecting Reasons to an Opinion" (page 18). Review the transition words in the word box at the bottom of "Connecting Reasons to an Opinion." *Read the sentences in Part One. Draw a box around the transition word in each sentence. Then write your topic sentence in Part Two. Think about your reasons for your opinion. Work with a partner to write reasons for your opinion. Use transition words from the word box.*

➤ Review

Review students' sentences to check for correct use of transition words and that their sentences make sense.

➤ Closing

You have learned how writers use transition words to connect reasons with an opinion. Then you practiced writing sentences with transition words.

➤ Answers

"Connecting Reasons to an Opinion" (page 18): 1. and; 2. when; 3. since; 4. because; 5. Then, because

Name(s): _____

Connecting Reasons to an Opinion

➤ **Part One**

Draw a box around the transition word in each sentence.

1. Salad is a healthy and interesting food.

2. Salad is delicious when it has the right things in it.

3. I add shredded carrots to my salad since they add extra flavor.

4. I don't use creamy dressing because it is higher in fat.

5. Then I enjoy eating my nachos because I know I made them healthy!

➤ **Part Two**

1. What is your opinion about your topic? Write your topic sentence below.

   _____

   _____

   _____

2. Why do you think this about your topic? Think about your reasons. Work with a partner to write reasons for your opinion. Use transition words from the box at the bottom of this page.

   _____

   _____

   _____

3. Read your sample sentences from "Reasons for My Opinion" (page 16) for ideas.

4. Look at your sensory words on "Descriptive Words" (page 15) to write new reasons to explain your opinion.

   _____

   _____

   _____

| also | and | because | but | if | since | so | then | when |

Concluding Sentences

➤ Objective

Students will learn about different purposes for a concluding sentence, practice rewriting topic sentences to restate opinions, and write concluding sentences for their opinion paragraphs.

➤ Introduction

You will practice rewriting topic sentences to state an opinion in a new way. You will also learn different purposes of a concluding sentence. Then you will write a concluding sentence for your opinion paragraph about an interesting healthy food.

➤ Instruction

The concluding sentence in an opinion paragraph says the writer's opinion about the topic in a different way. It also reviews the main idea for readers. The author may say that readers should agree with his or her opinion. Sometimes the author will suggest readers do something after reading the paragraph. A concluding sentence may have a word or phrase from the topic sentence. The concluding sentence is the author's final thought about the topic. It ties the whole paragraph together.

➤ Guided Practice

Distribute "Different Opinions" (page 20). Read the first four sentences aloud, one sentence at a time. *What is the topic in this sentence? What is the author's opinion? How could we rewrite this sentence to say the same thing in a different way?* Conduct a shared-writing activity to generate a concluding sentence for each topic in the sample sentences. *Why should readers agree with this opinion? What reason can we give?* Discuss. *Work with a classmate to rewrite the last two topic sentences in Part One on a separate piece of paper. Write each sentence as a concluding sentence that restates the opinion. Read your concluding sentences to others. Ask for thumbs-up/thumbs-down feedback on how well your sentence convinces readers to change the way they think. Then complete Part Two.*

➤ Independent Practice

Distribute "Delightful Dip" (page 21) and highlighters. *Read the paragraph with a partner. Highlight the concluding sentence. Then read the numbered sentences. Write a check mark next to any sentence that is true about the concluding sentence of the paragraph you read. Think about the topic of your opinion paragraph. What do you plan to say about it? Which of these ideas would work best for a concluding sentence for your opinion paragraph? Write a concluding sentence for your opinion paragraph.*

➤ Review

Review the possible purposes of a concluding sentence as listed on "Delightful Dip" before students practice writing their concluding sentences. Help students understand that they are to try to model at least one suggested purpose.

➤ Closing

You worked with classmates to rewrite topic sentences as concluding sentences. Then you practiced writing a concluding sentence for your own opinion paragraph.

➤ Answers

"Different Opinions" (page 20): 1. oatmeal, an interesting and healthy food for breakfast; 2. nachos, a healthy food for kids; 3. salad, favorite has interesting foods; 4. fish, eat it different ways; 5. pizza, is best with vegetables; 6. fruit, is a great healthy snack

"Delightful Dip" (page 21): check marks—1, 2, 3, 5 ("enchanting"/"great" are similar words)

Different Opinions

➤ Part One

What is the topic and author's opinion in each sentence? On a separate piece of paper, rewrite the last two topic sentences in your own words.

1. Oatmeal is an interesting and healthy food to have for breakfast. _____

_____

2. Nachos are a healthy food for kids to eat. _____

_____

3. My favorite kind of salad has interesting foods in it. _____

_____

4. I like to eat fish because I can eat it fixed different ways. _____

_____

5. The best way to have pizza is with lots of vegetables on it. _____

_____

6. Fruit makes a great healthy snack any time of day. _____

_____

➤ Part Two

1. Think about your topic sentence. Copy it here to help you remember your opinion about the topic.

_____

_____

2. Read the words authors sometimes use to tell their opinions to readers. What other opinion words do you know? Write them on the empty lines in the box.

believe	best	favorite	feel	good	great (greatest)
like	opinion	think	_____	_____	

3. Which opinion word did you use in your topic sentence? _____

4. How could you write your opinion a different way? _____

_____

Delightful Dip

Read the paragraph with a partner. Then highlight the concluding sentence.

Hummus is an enchanting dip when served with vegetables. By itself, it tastes almost bland. The thick, creamy paste is a little sweet and salty. It is sold in grocery stores. Hummus is a healthy food with a lot of protein. People dip carrots and celery in hummus. Cucumbers and tomatoes also taste good with hummus. It does not take very much to make a filling snack. Whoever created this dip did the impossible. Plain, raw vegetables taste great with a plain-looking dip!

A concluding sentence may have one or more purposes. Make a check mark by any statements that are true about the concluding sentence of the paragraph you read.

☐ **1.** The concluding sentence restates the author's opinion about the topic.

☐ **2.** The concluding sentence reviews the main idea for readers.

☐ **3.** The concluding sentence convinces readers to agree with the author's opinion.

☐ **4.** The concluding sentence asks readers to do something.

☐ **5.** The concluding sentence has a word or phrase from the topic sentence.

Practice writing a concluding sentence for your opinion paragraph about an interesting healthy food.

_____

_____

_____

What does your concluding sentence try to do?

_____

_____

Highlight the purpose in the list above that best matches your concluding sentence.

Teacher Notes

Grade level: above

Lexile estimate: 700L

First Draft and Peer Review

➤ Objective

Students will write the first drafts of their opinion paragraphs and participate in a peer review to clarify their writing.

➤ Introduction

Today you will write a first draft of your opinion paragraph about an interesting healthy food. You will use your writing from previous lessons. You will use your topic sentence from "Writing a Topic Sentence" (page 13). Then you will talk about your writing with a partner.

➤ Instruction

Authors write a first draft to put together all of their ideas for their opinion paragraphs. They write topic sentences and add the reasons that explain their opinions. Then they write concluding sentences to make complete paragraphs. As you write your first draft, write your sentences in an order that makes sense. This will help readers follow what you want to say. Review and role-play how to offer positive and constructive feedback on classmates' writing.

➤ Guided Practice

To write your first draft, combine the drafts and writing you have done in previous activities into one paragraph. Ensure students have their copies of "Writing a Topic Sentence." *Begin with the topic sentence that you wrote. Look at the reasons you wrote on "Reasons for My Opinion" (page 16). Then review the sentences you wrote with transition words on "Connecting Reasons to an Opinion" (page 18). Read the sample concluding sentences you wrote on "Different Opinions" (page 20) and "Delightful Dip" (page 21). Add the sentence that fits best with your paragraph.*

➤ Independent Practice

Distribute "Read and Respond" (page 23). *Read your partner's opinion paragraph. Circle five words that stand out to you. Why do you like these words? How do these words describe the topic? How do these words explain the writer's opinion? Talk about your answers with your partner. Then write three questions you have about your partner's writing. You might ask your partner a question about the topic. You might ask your partner to explain his or her opinion more. You can also write a question about a reason you don't understand.*

➤ Review

Provide examples of words that describe a topic, for example, from "Descriptive Words" (page 15). Discuss with students how descriptive words can help explain an author's opinion.

➤ Closing

Today you wrote a first draft of your opinion piece. Then you read a partner's writing. In the next lesson, you will write a second draft.

Name(s): _____

Read and Respond

➤ Part One

Read your partner's opinion paragraph about an interesting healthy food. Circle the five words you like best in your partner's paragraph.

1. Why do you like these words? _____

_____

2. How do these words describe the topic? _____

_____

3. How do these words explain the author's opinion? _____

_____

Talk about your answers with your partner.

➤ Part Two

Write three questions for your partner about his or her writing.

1. _____

_____

2. _____

_____

3. _____

_____

Trade papers with your partner and answer your partner's questions about your opinion paragraph.

1. _____

_____

2. _____

_____

3. _____

_____

Work with your partner to write one or two things you want to change on your first draft.

Second Draft and Self-Evaluation

➤ Objective

Students will write the second drafts of their opinion paragraphs and conduct self-evaluations using a rubric.

➤ Introduction

You will reread your first draft. Then you will use your notes to write a second draft of your opinion paragraph. You will use a chart called a rubric. It will help you think about your writing and make changes when you write a second draft.

➤ Instruction

You have written a first draft of your opinion paragraph and talked about your writing with a classmate. Next, authors write a second draft. They look at notes they have written about changes they would like to make to their writing. You will also use a rubric to help you write a second draft. A rubric is a chart that describes strong and weak writing. For example, the rubric you will use talks about conventions. A convention is the way we usually do something in English. When we use correct spelling, capitalization, and punctuation, our writing is easier to read and understand. The rubric shows that writing with correct conventions would receive a score of 4.

➤ Guided Practice

Distribute "What I Notice About My Writing" (page 25). *Use this page to think about your first draft. Whisper-read your paragraph. Then complete the graphic organizer for each part of your writing. Use the notes you have written on the graphic organizer. Look also at your first draft and your partner's feedback on "Read and Respond" (page 23). Then write a second draft of your opinion paragraph.*

➤ Independent Practice

It is important to look carefully at our writing. We look to see what is good and valuable in it. You will use a rubric to help you think about what makes strong opinion writing. It's also important to note areas in which we are still learning and need more practice. Distribute "Self-Evaluation: Opinion Paragraph" (page 26). *This chart shows what I will look for in your writing when I read your opinion paragraphs. Look at this page as you read your second draft. Circle the description for each part of an opinion paragraph that best matches your writing.*

➤ Review

Discuss the impact revising has on the writing process. Review specific categories of the rubric, as needed, to guide students as they write their second drafts.

➤ Closing

Today you made your writing better by looking at a rubric. You used your notes and comments you have received to write a second draft of your opinion paragraph about an interesting healthy food. The rubric and the comments helped you write a stronger second draft.

Name(s): _____

What I Notice About My Writing

Whisper-read your first draft. Complete the graphic organizer to make sure each part of your paragraph is exactly the way you want it.

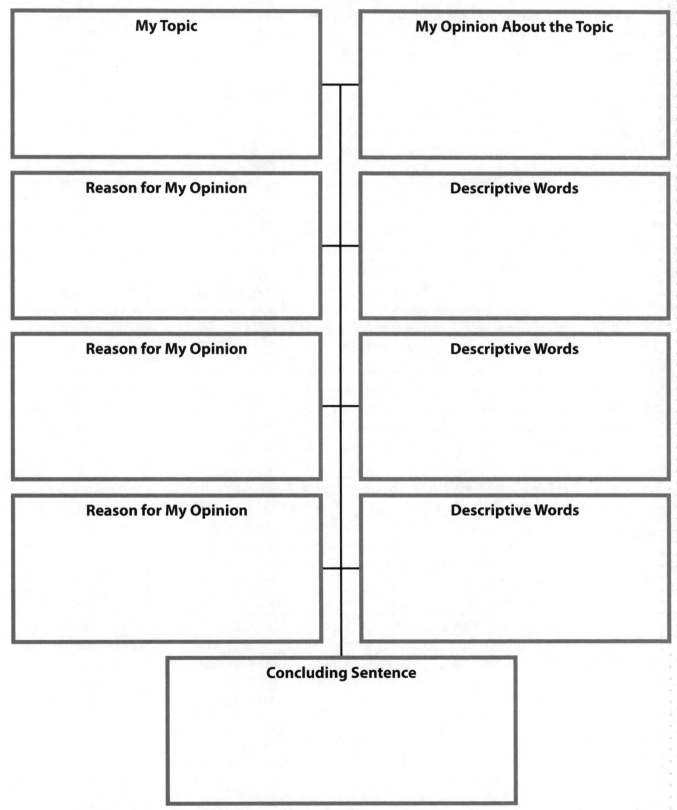

My Topic	My Opinion About the Topic

Reason for My Opinion	Descriptive Words

Reason for My Opinion	Descriptive Words

Reason for My Opinion	Descriptive Words

Concluding Sentence

Self-Evaluation: Opinion Paragraph

Name: _____   **Score:** _____

	4	3	2	1
Topic Sentence— Topic	My topic sentence clearly introduces an interesting healthy food.	My topic sentence introduces a topic about an interesting healthy food.	My topic sentence introduces a topic.	My paragraph does not have a topic sentence, or it is not about a specific topic.
Topic Sentence— Opinion	My topic sentence includes my opinion about the same interesting healthy food.	My topic sentence includes my opinion about an interesting healthy food.	My topic sentence includes an opinion.	My topic sentence does not include an opinion.
Reasons	My paragraph has reasons that clearly explain my opinion about an interesting healthy food.	My paragraph has reasons that relate to my opinion about an interesting healthy food.	My paragraph has reasons for an opinion.	My paragraph does not have reasons that support an opinion.
Details and Descriptive Words	My paragraph has supporting details that include descriptive words.	My paragraph has details that describe an interesting healthy food.	My paragraph has descriptive words.	My paragraph does not have descriptive words or details about the topic.
Transition Words	I use transition words correctly to clearly connect my reasons to my opinion about an interesting healthy food.	I use transition words to connect my reasons to my opinion about an interesting healthy food.	I use a few transition words to connect reasons to my opinion.	I do not use any transition words to connect reasons to an opinion.
Concluding Sentence	My paragraph has a concluding sentence that directly relates to the topic and restates my opinion about an interesting healthy food.	My paragraph has a concluding sentence that restates my opinion about an interesting healthy food.	My paragraph has a concluding sentence about the topic or my opinion.	My paragraph does not have a concluding sentence.
Conventions	I use correct spelling, capitalization, and punctuation in my paragraph.	I use correct spelling, capitalization, and punctuation most of the time in my paragraph.	I use some correct spelling, capitalization, and punctuation in my paragraph.	I had trouble using correct spelling, capitalization, and punctuation in my paragraph.

Final Draft

➤ Objective

Students will read and discuss the second drafts of their opinion paragraphs to make final revisions. They will also review a checklist for conventions and then write final drafts of their paragraphs.

➤ Introduction

In the last lesson, you wrote a second draft of your opinion paragraph. Today you will read and talk about your draft with a classmate. You will plan one thing you want to change to make your writing even better. You will also look at a checklist. It will remind you to think about correct conventions in your writing. Then you will write a final draft of your paragraph.

➤ Instruction

Authors change their writing before they write final drafts. They make them stronger and easier for readers to understand. Sometimes details need to be added to help explain the authors' reasons for their opinions. The writing may have extra words that need to be taken out. Authors may change some words to make them more exact. It is important to check to make sure that sentences are in an order that makes sense.

➤ Guided Practice

Distribute "Revising My Opinion Paragraph" (page 28). *Read the second draft of your opinion paragraph aloud to a classmate. Then read the questions and talk about your answers. Think about changes you can make to your writing to make it easier to read and understand. Choose one thing you will change in your paragraph. In the box in Part One, write about how you will change your writing to make it better.*

➤ Independent Practice

Review the conventions listed in the chart in Part Two of "Revising My Opinion Paragraph." *Read the second draft of your paragraph several times. Then check your paragraph for each convention. Correct any mistakes you find. Place a check mark in the first column next to each convention as you correct it. Read your notes on your second draft. Look at the corrections you have made. Then write a final draft of your opinion paragraph about an interesting healthy food.*

➤ Review

Monitor and encourage students as they write their final drafts. Remind them to incorporate revisions and corrections from their second drafts as they write.

➤ Closing

Today you read through your second draft and made corrections. Then you used your notes to write a final draft of your opinion paragraph. Now it is ready for an audience.

Name(s): _____

Revising My Opinion Paragraph

➤ Part One

1. Read the second draft of your opinion paragraph aloud to a classmate.

2. Then read the questions below and talk about your writing.
   - What could you add to your writing to make it easier to understand?
   - What extra words should you take out?
   - Which words could be changed to use a more descriptive word?
   - What words or sentences should be in a different order to make better sense?
   - Which change will be the hardest for you to make? Which is the easiest?

3. Choose one way you would like to make your writing stronger. Write what you will do in the box below.

➤ Part Two

1. Read the second draft of your paragraph several times.

2. Check your paragraph for each convention. Make any corrections your writing needs.

3. Place a check mark in the first column next to each convention as you check and correct it.

	I used plural nouns correctly.
	I used adjectives correctly to describe nouns.
	I used adverbs correctly to describe verbs.
	I used past-tense verb tenses correctly.
	I used a variety of sentence patterns.
	My sentences make sense.
	I used capitalization correctly.
	My sentences have correct ending punctuation.
	I spelled words correctly.
	I used words and phrases that mean exactly what I want to say.

Final Evaluation

➤ Objective

Students will observe a demonstration of how the teacher uses a rubric to score student writing and participate in a class discussion. Then they will use a chart to compare the scores they gave their writing with the scores they received from the teacher and answer response questions.

➤ Introduction

You have used a chart called a rubric to look closely at your writing. Today you will receive scores from me. I will use a chart that looks very similar. You will compare the two scores to notice what you did well. You will also think about how you can continue to make your writing stronger.

➤ Instruction

In these lessons, you have talked about your writing with classmates. How does getting comments from a classmate help you improve your writing? You also used a rubric to look closely at your writing. The rubric described strong opinion writing. Stronger writing receives higher scores on the point scale. Reading each level helps us know how we can make our writing better. Display "Teacher Evaluation: Opinion Paragraph" (page 30). *How does the rubric describe each area of opinion writing?*

➤ Guided Practice

Display a sample opinion paragraph, for example, "Healthy Nachos" (page 6). *How would you score each part of this paragraph on the rubric?* Take notes of student scores and then model how you would score the paragraph using the rubric. *Which areas did I score differently? Why do you think there are differences?* (The teacher has a different perspective and more experience.) *What can we learn from looking at each set of scores?* (A student could focus on one area and read the descriptions to plan one specific thing to change and try to do better.)

➤ Independent Practice

Distribute students' copies of "Teacher Evaluation: Opinion Paragraph," students' completed self-evaluations ("Self-Evaluation: Opinion Paragraph" [page 26]), "Learning from Differences" (page 31), and green or blue crayons or pencils. *Read the chart at the top of "Learning from Differences." Compare the scores you gave yourself with the scores I gave your paragraph. Reread your paragraph and then answer the questions on the bottom part of the page.*

➤ Review

Review and discuss possible responses to the questions on "Learning from Differences." Discuss ways students use their writing strengths to help classmates as well as ways they could improve specific aspects by following the guidelines suggested by the wording on the rubric.

➤ Closing

We talked together in class about how I use a rubric to score your writing. Then you compared the scores I gave you with the scores you gave your writing.

Teacher Evaluation: Opinion Paragraph

Student Name: _____   **Score:** _____

	4	3	2	1
Topic Sentence— Topic	The topic sentence clearly introduces an interesting healthy food.	The topic sentence introduces a topic about an interesting healthy food.	The topic sentence introduces a topic.	The paragraph does not have a topic sentence, or it is not about a specific topic.
Topic Sentence— Opinion	The topic sentence includes the author's opinion about the same interesting healthy food.	The topic sentence includes the author's opinion about an interesting healthy food.	The topic sentence includes an opinion.	The topic sentence does not include an opinion.
Reasons	The paragraph has reasons that clearly explain the author's opinion about an interesting healthy food.	The paragraph has reasons that relate to the author's opinion about an interesting healthy food.	The paragraph has reasons for an opinion.	The paragraph does not have reasons that support an opinion.
Details and Descriptive Words	The paragraph has supporting details that include descriptive words.	The paragraph has details that describe an interesting healthy food.	The paragraph has descriptive words.	The paragraph does not have descriptive words or details about the topic.
Transition Words	The author uses transition words correctly to clearly connect reasons to his or her opinion about an interesting healthy food.	The author uses transition words to connect reasons to his or her opinion about an interesting healthy food.	The author uses a few transition words to connect reasons to his or her opinion.	The author does not use transition words to connect reasons to an opinion.
Concluding Sentence	The paragraph has a concluding sentence that directly relates to the topic and restates the author's opinion about an interesting healthy food.	The paragraph has a concluding sentence that restates the author's opinion about an interesting healthy food.	The paragraph has a concluding sentence about the topic or the author's opinion.	The paragraph does not have a concluding sentence.
Conventions	The author uses correct spelling, capitalization, and punctuation in the paragraph.	The author uses correct spelling, capitalization, and punctuation most of the time in the paragraph.	The author uses some correct spelling, capitalization, and punctuation in the paragraph.	The author has trouble using correct spelling, capitalization, and punctuation in the paragraph.

Learning from Differences

1. In the second column, write the score you gave yourself on "Self-Evaluation: Opinion Paragraph" (page 26) for each part of your opinion paragraph.

2. In the third column, write the score you received in each area on "Teacher Evaluation: Opinion Paragraph" (page 30).

Characteristics of Opinion/Argumentative Writing	My Score	Teacher's Score
The topic sentence introduces a topic.		
The topic sentence includes the author's opinion.		
Reasons explain the author's opinion.		
Supporting details include descriptive words.		
Transition words connect reasons to the opinion.		
The concluding sentence restates the topic and opinion.		
Correct spelling, capitalization, and punctuation are used.		

3. Use a green pencil or crayon to circle the highest score you received from the teacher. How does that score compare to the score you gave yourself for the same quality?

_____

_____

4. Use a blue pencil or crayon to circle a low score from the teacher you would like to improve. How does that score compare to the score you gave yourself for the same quality?

_____

_____

5. Look at the quality your teacher scored the highest. How could you help classmates learn about or improve their writing in this area?

_____

_____

6. Think about the quality you circled to improve. What is one thing you could do to make your writing stronger in that area?

_____

_____

Review

➤ Objective

Students will read a sample opinion paragraph and review qualities of opinion writing illustrated in the paragraph. They will also write their own opinions of the topic based on the author's reasons.

➤ Introduction

You will read an example of an opinion paragraph. Then we will talk about how the paragraph is an example of opinion writing. You will list each feature of opinion writing you notice in the paragraph. Then you will think about the author's reasons for his or her opinion. You will write your own opinion on the subject of the paragraph.

➤ Instruction

In this module, you have learned what makes strong opinion writing. Opinion writing tells what the author thinks or believes about something. The topic sentence introduces the subject. It tells the author's opinion about the topic. Opinion writing uses descriptive words to give reasons for the author's opinion. A concluding sentence restates the topic and author's opinion.

➤ Guided Practice

Display "A Fruit for All Tastes" (page 33). Conduct a popcorn-style read-aloud activity to include as many students as possible. *What do you notice about this opinion paragraph? What makes it an example of strong opinion writing?* Encourage students to list qualities from the Instruction above. *Which of the five senses does the author include? Why does the author think this way about the topic? What are the author's reasons for his or her opinion? Which sentences do not seem to connect to the opinion? What do you think about the concluding sentence?*

➤ Independent Practice

Distribute "A Fruit for All Tastes" and "My Opinion Counts" (page 34). *Read the paragraph. Copy each part of the paragraph into the correct part of the triangle. Look at the author's reasons. Do you agree or disagree with the author's opinion? How did the author's reasons help you decide whether you agree or disagree? Circle the reasons you listed from the paragraph that help you form your opinion. Then write your opinion of the topic in the box.*

➤ Review

Discuss how the reasons in the paragraph influenced students' responses as they completed "My Opinion Counts." Encourage students to practice using descriptive details to share other reasons they have for their opinions of the provided topic.

➤ Closing

You read an example of opinion writing. Then you wrote the words and sentences from the paragraph that match each part of an opinion paragraph. You also used the author's reasons to think about your own opinion of the topic.

➤ Answers

"My Opinion Counts" (page 34): *topic*—pineapple; *author's opinion*—is a great tasting healthy food; *reasons*—it is sweet, it goes with many things (inferred), there are many ways to eat pineapple.

Name(s): _____

A Fruit for All Tastes

Pineapple is a great tasting healthy food! It is good in fruit salads. It is also good for dinner. Pineapple grows on tropical trees. People buy it in grocery stores around summertime. Pineapple can be grilled in large cubes with meat and vegetables. The sweetness of the pineapple is different than the taste of the grilled food. Some people like to eat pineapple with rice. A round slice of pineapple will fit on a hamburger. Pineapple is a sweet fruit. The middle of the pineapple is called the core. The fruit can be used in fruit smoothies for an after-dinner dessert. Some people like to drink pineapple juice. It is good mixed with orange juice. Pineapple juice is also used to make sorbet. Sorbet is like ice cream, but it is made with fruit juice instead of milk. No matter how you eat pineapple, it is a delicious summer fruit!

Teacher Notes

Grade level: appropriate
Lexile estimate: 530L

Name(s): _____

My Opinion Counts

1. Read "A Fruit for All Tastes" (page 33).

2. Copy each part of the paragraph in the correct part of the triangle below.

3. Do you agree or disagree with the author's opinion?

4. Circle the reasons you listed from the paragraph that help you form your opinion.

5. Write your opinion of the topic in the box below the triangle.

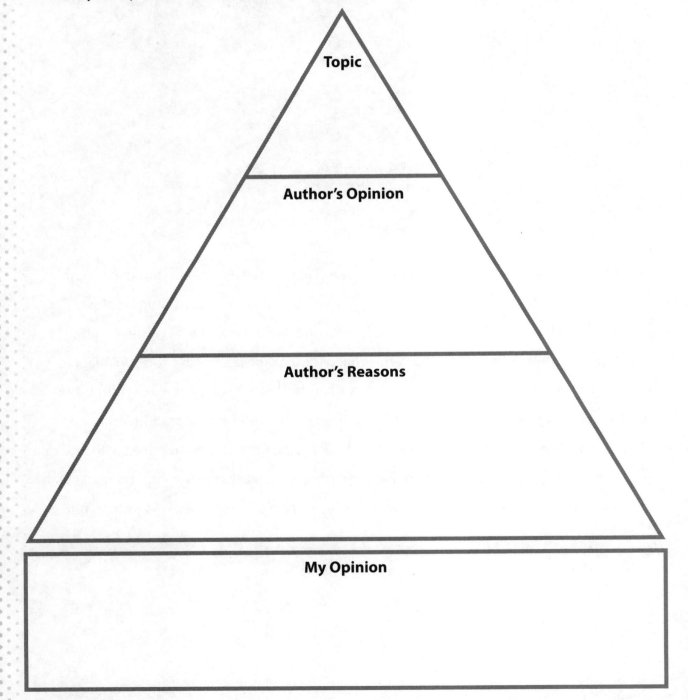

Introductory Paragraphs

➤ Objective
Students will identify the topics and opinions in sample thesis statements. They will ask and answer questions to gather ideas about the module topic and then use a web diagram to plan their opinion essays.

➤ Introduction
You will learn about thesis statements and talk with classmates to learn their ideas about a topic. Then you will choose a topic and think about your opinion on that subject. You will brainstorm reasons for your opinion to begin planning your opinion essay. Our topic for this module is school clothes.

➤ Instruction
A longer piece of opinion writing might have more than one paragraph. The first paragraph is called the introductory paragraph. In this paragraph, the topic sentence is also called the thesis statement. The thesis statement introduces the topic and gives your opinion about the topic. This statement may be the first sentence. The introductory paragraph also sums up the reasons for the opinion.

➤ Guided Practice
Display "What Is a Thesis Statement?" (page 36) and call on students to read the sample thesis statements, one at a time. *What do you notice about these sentences?* (They are thesis statements with a stated topic and author's opinion.) *What is the topic in these sentences?* Have volunteers mark the text. *We will draw a box around the topic in each sentence. What are the author's opinions about the topic? Let's underline the opinions. What reasons do you think the author will give to explain why he or she has these opinions?* Discuss and invite students to contribute reasons verbally or in writing. *How can studying these model sentences help you write your own thesis statement?*

Distribute "Learning About a Topic" (page 37). *What do you think about school clothes? Sometimes hearing other peoples' ideas helps us to form our own opinions. Write three questions you will ask classmates about school clothes. Work with your small group to ask and answer your questions.*

➤ Independent Practice
Distribute "Planning My Essay" (page 38). *In the top circle in Part One, write your topic.* Suggest possible topics from "Writing Topics" (page 155). *Think about the ideas you have heard from your classmates, friends, teachers, and family members about your topic. In the center circle, write your opinion about your topic. What are some reasons for your opinion? Write ideas in the other circles on the web. Then, for Part Two, write a thesis statement.*

➤ Review
Review the characteristics of an effective introductory paragraph for an opinion essay. As time allows, suggest students draft an introductory paragraph based on the ideas they generated on "Planning My Essay."

➤ Closing
Today you learned about introductory paragraphs and thesis statements. You asked classmates about their ideas about the topic. Then you chose your own topic and thought about the reasons for your opinion about that topic. You also wrote your own thesis statement.

➤ Answers
"What Is a Thesis Statement?" (page 36): 1. The best school clothes are easy to wash; 2. I think it is a good idea for kids to wear the same kind of clothes to school; 3. Kids should have a choice in what they wear to school; 4. School uniforms keep kids safe; 5. My opinion is that school uniforms would cost too much money; 6. I would love not to have to decide what to wear each day.

Name(s): _____

What Is a Thesis Statement?

> What is the **topic** in each sentence? (Box it.)
>
> What is the **author's opinion** about the topic? (Underline it.)
>
> What **reasons** might support this opinion? (Write them.)

1. The best school clothes are easy to wash.

   _____

   _____

2. I think it is a good idea for kids to wear the same kind of clothes to school.

   _____

   _____

3. Kids should have a choice in what they wear to school.

   _____

   _____

4. School uniforms keep kids safe.

   _____

   _____

5. My opinion is that school uniforms would cost too much money.

   _____

   _____

6. I would love not having to decide what to wear each day.

   _____

   _____

Name(s): _____

Learning About a Topic

1. On the lines below, write three questions you want to ask classmates about school clothes.

2. Write the ideas and answers you receive from your classmates in the boxes below each question.

A. _____

_____

_____

B. _____

_____

_____

C. _____

_____

_____

Name(s): _____

Planning My Essay

➤ Part One

1. Write your topic in the top circle.

2. Write your opinion in the center oval.

3. What are some reasons for your opinion? Write your ideas in the other circles on the web. (*Note:* You may not be able to fill every reason circle.)

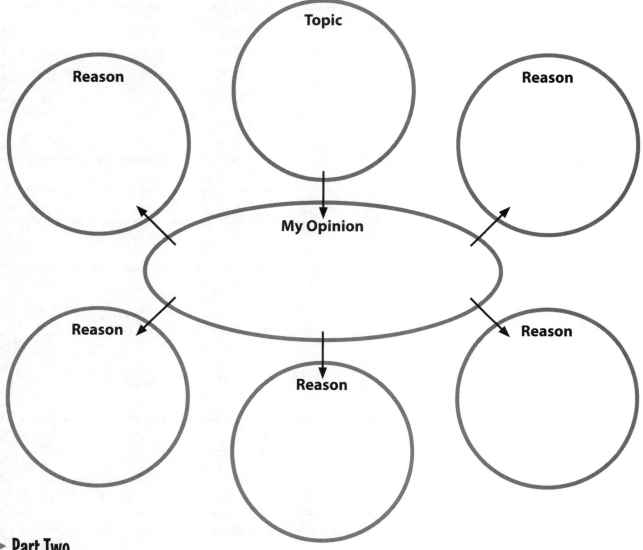

➤ Part Two

Write your thesis statement below.

_____

_____

Body Paragraphs

➤ Objective

Students will brainstorm descriptive words, share them with partners, and discuss the role of descriptive words as a class. They will also list reasons for their opinions and practice using transition words to connect their reasons with their opinions.

➤ Introduction

You will brainstorm descriptive words to use when explaining the reasons for your opinion. Then you will share and discuss your words with classmates. You will also write reasons that support your opinion. Then you will practice using transition words to connect the reasons to your opinion.

➤ Instruction

Each paragraph in the body of your essay explains and supports one of the reasons introduced in the introductory paragraph. These paragraphs contain facts and details that connect to the reasons. Descriptive words tell readers about your topic and why you think a certain way about that topic. Include examples to show readers why your opinion makes sense. Ask yourself, "How can I explain my reasons so readers will understand?" Remember to use transition words to connect your reasons with your opinion.

➤ Guided Practice

Distribute "Describing My Topic" (page 40). *Think about your topic. What words describe the topic and your opinion? Which descriptive words could you use to explain the reasons for your opinion? Brainstorm descriptive words and write them in the oval. Include facts and details that relate to your reasons.*

Share your words with a partner. Add any additional words you and your partner think of to the rhombus. Which words would you like to share with classmates to help them think about how to explain their reasons to readers? Discuss students' responses and how descriptive words can move readers to respond to an opinion, by agreeing with it or considering a change in behavior as a result of reading the opinion and reasons. If desired, create a class-generated web of descriptive words related to the module topic.

➤ Independent Practice

Distribute "Explaining My Opinion" (page 41). *List reasons that explain your opinion on the shape. Use the words you brainstormed on "Describing My Topic" for ideas. What examples can you include that will help readers understand your reasons?*

We use transition words to connect reasons with our opinion. Read the transition words in the box. Then circle any transition words you used when you wrote your reasons. If your reason sentences do not have transition words, rewrite one or two sentences. Use a transition word from the word box that will help connect each reason to your opinion.

➤ Review

Review how to use transition words correctly in sentences to connect reasons to an opinion.

➤ Closing

You used descriptive words to write reasons that support and explain your opinion about your topic. You also practiced writing sentences with transition words.

Describing My Topic

➤ **Part One**

Write your thesis statement in the box below.

[ ]

In the oval below, write words that describe your topic and your opinion about that topic. Include facts and details that relate to your reasons.

( )

➤ **Part Two**

Share your descriptive words with a partner. Work together to use a dictionary to find other words that will help you explain your reasons to readers. Write the new words in the rhombus below.

< >

➤ **Part Three**

Share your descriptive words with the class.

Name(s): _____

Explaining My Opinion

1. List reasons that explain your opinion on the burst below. Use words from "Describing My Topic" (page 40) to describe and explain the reasons that support your opinion. What examples can you include that will help readers understand your reasons?

2. Read the transition words in the box below.

| also | and | because | but | if | since | so | then |

3. Circle any transition words that you used when you wrote your reasons.

4. If your reason sentences do not have transition words, rewrite one or two sentences and include a transition word from the box above.

_____

_____

_____

_____

_____

Concluding Paragraphs

➤ Objective

Students will share opinions and discuss the significance of those opinions for readers, then they will complete a series of guided steps to draft concluding paragraphs for their opinion essays.

➤ Introduction

Today you will discuss with classmates why readers will want to read your opinion. Then you will follow a series of steps to practice writing a concluding paragraph for your opinion essay about school clothes.

➤ Instruction

The concluding paragraph in an opinion essay restates the topic and author's opinion. It will summarize the reasons for the opinion. A concluding paragraph may tell why the opinion matters to readers. The author may also say why readers should agree with his or her opinion or should take action.

➤ Guided Practice

Distribute "Our Opinions Matter" (page 43) and conduct a "Give One, Get One" activity. *What is your opinion about school clothes? Write your opinion in the top box in the left column on the chart. Share your opinion with a classmate. Ask your classmate the question in the second column. Write your classmate's response in the box. Then listen as your classmate shares his or her opinion. Write it in the bottom part of the left column. Think about how you would answer the question about your classmate's opinion. Write your answer in the last box and share it with your classmate.* Have students repeat the process with one or more classmates if they have time.

➤ Independent Practice

Distribute "How to Write a Concluding Paragraph" (page 44) along with students' copies of "Planning My Essay" (page 38) and "Explaining My Opinion" (page 41). Guide students through summarizing their topics, opinions, and reasons to write concluding paragraphs for their opinion essays. *Think about the topic and opinion you included in your thesis statement. Then write a new sentence that restates your topic and opinion about that topic. Read the reasons for your opinion and write one or two words that describe each main point in your essay. Write one sentence that combines these main ideas from your essay. This sentence will be a summary or overview of the reasons for your opinion. Write one more sentence to end your essay. Try to convince readers to agree with your opinion. Consider all the sample sentences you just wrote. Then write your concluding paragraph on a separate piece of paper.*

➤ Review

Review with students how to restate their topics and opinions, and what it means to summarize their reasons into one sentence. Read samples of interesting concluding sentences that engage readers as a model for students.

➤ Closing

You discussed with classmates why readers would want to read your opinion. You also thought about ways to encourage readers to agree with your opinion. Then you wrote a concluding paragraph for your essay.

Name(s): _____

Our Opinions Matter

1. Write your opinion in the top half of the first column.

2. Share your opinion with a classmate.

3. Write your classmate's answer to the question in the top half of the second column.

4. Write your classmate's opinion in the bottom half of the first column.

5. Share why you think your classmate's opinion is important. Write your response in the bottom half of the second column.

My Opinion	Why is this idea important?
Classmate's Opinion	**Why is this idea important?**

Name(s): _____

How to Write a Concluding Paragraph

1. Think about your topic and opinion from the thesis statement you wrote on "Planning My Essay" (page 38).

2. Write a new sentence that tells your topic and opinion about that topic.

   _____

   _____

   _____

3. Read the reasons for your opinion you wrote on "Explaining My Opinion" (page 41).

4. Write one or two words that describe each main point on each exclamation point below.

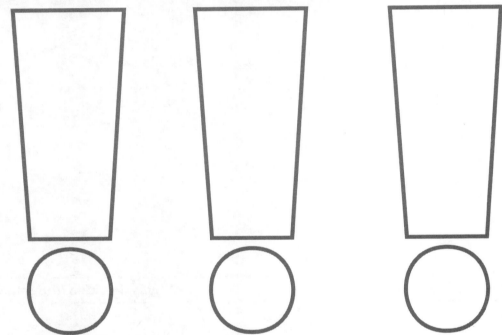

5. Write one sentence that combines these main ideas from your essay. This sentence will be a summary of the reasons for your opinion.

   _____

   _____

6. Write one more sentence to end your essay. What can you say to try to get readers to agree with your opinion?

   _____

   _____

7. Consider the responses above. Then write your concluding paragraph on a separate piece of paper.

First Draft and Peer Review

➤ Objective

Students will use a checklist to guide them as they write first drafts of their opinion essays and then use the same checklist to review and discuss partners' essays. They will also respond to prompts to give feedback to their partners.

➤ Introduction

You have already written notes and sentences in earlier lessons. Today you will use them to write a first draft of your opinion essay about a topic related to school clothes. You will also use a checklist to help you write. You will use the same checklist to review a partner's writing and give feedback to him or her.

➤ Instruction

Your first copy of your opinion essay will include all the parts you've worked on so far. Your draft will include an introductory paragraph. This first paragraph will have a thesis statement. Your thesis statement will tell readers your topic and your opinion about that topic. It will also introduce the reasons for your opinion. Each body paragraph will explain and support one reason with facts and details. Descriptive words will also help explain your reasons to readers. An opinion essay has transition words that connect reasons to the author's opinion. This helps readers understand why the author thinks this way about the topic. The concluding paragraph restates the topic and author's opinion. It summarizes the reasons for the opinion. An interesting closing sentence may show readers why the author's opinion is important. It may also tell readers why they should agree with the opinion.

➤ Guided Practice

Distribute "Opinion Essay Checklist" (page 46). *You will use a checklist to guide you as you write a first draft of your opinion essay. Each sentence on the checklist describes a feature that is part of strong opinion writing.* Ensure students have their copies of "Learning About a Topic" (page 37), "Planning My Essay" (page 38), "Describing My Topic" (page 40), "Explaining My Opinion" (page 41), "Our Opinions Matter" (page 43), and "How to Write a Concluding Paragraph" (page 44). *Use the notes you have already written to write your first draft. Then look back at the checklist to make sure you've included all of the parts of an opinion essay that make it easy for readers to understand it.*

➤ Independent Practice

Work with a partner to read and discuss your first drafts. Use the checklist to check your partner's essay. Then complete the sentences at the bottom of the page to give feedback to your partner.

➤ Review

Review the sentences on "Opinion Essay Checklist" to check for student understanding. Monitor students as they review classmates' writing using the checklist and clarify as necessary.

➤ Closing

Today you wrote a first draft of your opinion essay. You worked with a partner to give and receive feedback about your writing.

Name(s): _____

Opinion Essay Checklist

➤ Part One

Use the checklist below to guide you as you write your first draft. Then trade papers and read your partner's essay. Place a check mark in the column next to each quality included in his or her writing.

Introductory Paragraph	
	The thesis statement states the topic.
	The thesis statement gives the author's opinion about the topic.
	This first paragraph summarizes the reasons for the opinion.
Body Paragraphs	
	Each body paragraph explains one reason.
	Body paragraphs use descriptive words to explain the reason to readers.
	Body paragraphs include facts, details, and examples to explain the author's reasons.
	Transition words connect the reasons with the author's opinion.
Concluding Paragraph	
	This final paragraph says the topic and the author's opinion about that topic in a different way.
	This final paragraph summarizes the author's reasons for the opinion.
	This final paragraph has an interesting closing sentence that says why readers should agree with the author's opinion.

➤ Part Two

Complete the sentences to give your partner feedback about his or her opinion essay.

- My favorite part of your essay was _____ because

  _____.

- I read your thesis statement, and I think your opinion is _____

  _____.

- You could try to make your body paragraphs stronger by _____

  _____

  _____.

- The closing sentence in your concluding paragraph is interesting because _____

  _____.

Second Draft and Self-Evaluation

➤ Objective

In small groups, students will discuss their responses to questions about revising their writing, write second drafts of their opinion essays, and evaluate their second drafts using a rubric.

➤ Introduction

You will look at the comments you received from classmates. Then you will ask and answer questions with a small group. These questions will help you think about changes you would like to make to your first draft. Then you will write a second draft of your opinion essay. You will use a rubric to look at strengths and weaknesses in your writing.

➤ Instruction

You have used a checklist to write the first draft of your opinion essay. You also talked with a partner about your writing. You wrote notes about things you want to change to make your writing stronger. What does the author want to do in an opinion essay? (to get readers to agree to change the way they think or behave) Think about this reason for writing as you write a second draft. The second draft of your essay is not your final draft. You will look at a rubric to help you make more changes to your writing.

➤ Guided Practice

Look back at the comments a partner gave you on "Opinion Essay Checklist" (page 46). Display the following questions for student reference. Talk about your answers to these questions in a small group: How could you rewrite your thesis statement to make your opinion clear to readers? What is one thing you will do to make the body paragraphs in your essay easier to understand? How well do your reasons connect to your opinion? Take notes on your first draft about things you would like to change.

➤ Independent Practice

Use your notes from "Opinion Essay Checklist" and what you heard in your small group to write a second draft of your opinion essay. Distribute "Self-Evaluation: Opinion Essay" (page 48) and highlighters. A rubric is a chart that describes strong and weak writing. This rubric lists each part of an opinion essay on a different line. Highlight the score that best describes your writing for each part of your essay. What is one area in which you are happy with your writing? What is one thing you would like to make better?

➤ Review

Discuss the impact revising has on the writing process. Review specific categories of the rubric, as needed, to guide students as they write their final drafts. Model how to highlight one score description in each category or quality of an opinion essay.

➤ Closing

Look back at the rubric you highlighted and any notes you wrote on your second draft about changes you would like to make. Then write a final draft of your opinion essay to turn in to me. I will use a rubric like the one you used to score your essay.

Self-Evaluation: Opinion Essay

Name: _____   **Score:** _____

	4	3	2	1
Thesis Statement— Topic	My thesis statement clearly introduces a topic about school clothes.	My thesis statement introduces a topic about school clothes.	My thesis statement introduces a topic.	My introductory paragraph does not have a thesis statement, or it is not about a specific topic.
Thesis Statement— Opinion	My thesis statement clearly states my opinion about the same topic.	My thesis statement includes an opinion about the topic of school clothes.	My thesis statement includes an opinion.	My thesis statement does not include an opinion.
Body Paragraphs	Each body paragraph clearly explains one reason that supports my opinion about school clothes.	Each body paragraph explains a reason that relates to my opinion about school clothes.	Each body paragraph has a reason for my opinion.	My essay does not have body paragraphs, or they do not have reasons that support an opinion.
Descriptive Words and Details	My body paragraphs have supporting details that include descriptive words.	My body paragraphs have details that describe school clothes.	My body paragraphs have descriptive words.	My body paragraphs do not have descriptive words or details about the topic.
Transition Words	I use transition words correctly to clearly connect my reasons to my opinion about school clothes.	I use transition words to connect my reasons to my opinion about school clothes.	I use a few transition words to connect reasons to my opinion.	I do not use transition words to connect reasons to an opinion.
Concluding Paragraph	My essay has a concluding paragraph that directly relates to the topic and restates my opinion about school clothes.	My essay has a concluding paragraph that relates to the thesis statement or restates my opinion about school clothes.	My essay has a concluding paragraph about the topic or my opinion.	My essay does not have a concluding paragraph.
Conventions	I use correct spelling, capitalization, and punctuation in my essay.	I use correct spelling, capitalization, and punctuation most of the time in my essay.	I use some correct spelling, capitalization, and punctuation in my essay.	I had trouble using correct spelling, capitalization, and punctuation in my essay.

Answer the following questions on a separate piece of paper:

1. What is one area in which you are happy with your writing?

2. What is one area you would like to improve?

Review

➤ Objective

Students will read a sample essay and identify characteristics of an opinion essay. Then they will play a review game with partners.

➤ Introduction

You will read an example of an opinion essay. Then you will point out features of opinion writing in the essay. You will also play a review game with a partner.

➤ Instruction

Let's think about what we have learned about writing an opinion essay. Discuss. *The introductory paragraph has a thesis statement. This sentence states the topic and the author's opinion about the topic. The first paragraph also introduces the reasons the author has this opinion. Each body paragraph has descriptive words to explain and support one reason. Authors use transition words to connect reasons to their opinions. Body paragraphs should be in an order that makes sense. The concluding paragraph says the topic and author's opinion in a different way. It may have a closing sentence that tries to get readers to agree with the author's opinion.*

➤ Guided Practice

Display the cube diagram from "What's Your Choice?" (page 51). Then display "The Question of School Clothes" (page 50) and read together as a class, with different students reading selected portions of the sample essay. *Let's find the qualities of an opinion essay in this piece. What is the topic? What is the author's opinion? How do you know? What reasons does the author give for his or her opinion? What do you notice about the last paragraph in the essay? Which sentence tries to get readers to agree with the author's opinion? How do you know?* Invite students to use a pointer to identify each part of the sample essay or underline key sentences.

➤ Independent Practice

Distribute scissors, tape, "The Question of School Clothes," and "What's Your Choice?" *You will make a cube to play a review game with a partner. Cut out the cube on page 51. Fold on the dotted lines. Then tape the cube together. Take turns tossing the cube. Which part shows face up on the cube? Tell your partner the sentence from the essay that matches that part. For example, if the topic side of the cube is facing up, tell your partner the topic of the essay. For extra practice, play another game. Tell your partner the sentence from your essay that matches the part showing on the cube.*

➤ Review

Review the reasons presented in the sample essay. Discuss why the order makes sense, or how the reasons could be rearranged to more directly relate to the introductory paragraph.

➤ Closing

You read a sample opinion essay. Then we talked about how the author included qualities of opinion writing in the essay. You also played a game with a partner to review the parts of an opinion essay.

➤ Answers

"What's Your Choice?" (page 51): *topic*—what kids should wear to school; *author's opinion*—a dress code solves the question; *reason*—a dress code is not as strict as a uniform, everyone wears clothes that are similar, kids will not be teased; *reason*—without a dress code kids might wear clothes that are not safe or cannot be washed easily; *reason*—school uniforms cost money; *reason*—uniforms all look the same; *concluding sentence* (restatement of author's opinion)—The best answer for what kids should wear to school is to have a dress code.

The Question of School Clothes

A school dress code solves the question of what kids should wear to school. Some schools say everyone should wear a uniform. The clothes all look the same. Other places let kids wear whatever they want to school. A dress code has the best parts of both ideas.

A dress code is a set of rules. It says what kids can and cannot wear to school. But it is not as strict as a uniform. Everyone wears clothes that are similar. Kids will not tease each other about what they wear. A dress code might say that kids cannot wear T-shirts with weird sayings. T-shirts would have to be plain colors. No one would make fun of someone wearing a T-shirt.

Some schools do not have rules about what kids can wear to school. One child might wear better clothes than other kids. A shirt might have long ties. It would not be safe for P.E. or at recess. A child's clothes might not wash easily. He or she could get in trouble if something gets spilled during art or lunch. Different people have different ideas about what clothes kids should wear.

School uniforms cost money. Some families might not be able to pay for them. Families with a few kids would have to pay more money than families with only one child.

Uniforms all look the same. Kids don't get to wear what they like. For example, they can't wear their favorite colors.

School should be a safe place where kids are not teased for what they wear. Some types of clothing are safer and better for school. A dress code lets families choose the type of clothes they can afford. The best answer for what kids should wear to school is to have a dress code.

Teacher Notes

Grade level: appropriate

Lexile estimate: 530L

Name(s): _____

What's Your Choice?

➤ Part One

1. Read the labels on the cube drawing below.

2. Cut out the cube.

3. Fold on the dotted lines.

4. Tape the cube together.

Topic

Author's Opinion | **Reason** | **Reason** | **Reason**

Concluding Sentence

➤ Part Two

1. Take turns tossing the cube.

2. Tell your partner the sentence from the essay that says that part. For example, if the topic side of the cube is facing up, tell your partner the topic of the essay.

3. For extra practice, play another game. Tell your partner the sentence from *your* essay that says that part.

Final Evaluation

➤ Objective

Students will observe a think-aloud that demonstrates how the teacher uses a rubric to score student writing. Then they will compare the scores they gave their opinion essays with the scores they received from the teacher. Students will also consider audiences for their writing and participate in a whole-class teacher-student dialogue to better understand how rubrics provide feedback to writers.

➤ Introduction

We will talk about how I use a rubric to score a sample essay. Then you will look back at the scores you gave yourself on "Self-Evaluation: Opinion Essay" (page 48) and compare those scores with the scores I gave you. You will also think about who will read your writing.

➤ Instruction

You used a rubric, or chart, to help you make changes to your second draft. It described strengths and weaknesses for each part of an opinion essay. The rubric helped you look closely at your writing as you wrote your final draft. I have used a rubric that looks almost the same to score your opinion essay. I looked at one feature of opinion writing at a time in the essay. Then I read the descriptions listed on the rubric to see which most closely matches the writing in your essay. Now that you have written a final draft, it is time to think about who will read your writing.

➤ Guided Practice

Display "The Question of School Clothes" (page 50) and "Teacher Evaluation: Opinion Essay" (page 53). Model and think aloud to show how you would score the sample essay. *The first two lines of the rubric describe the thesis statement.* Read aloud the thesis statement and the descriptions for scores 1–4. *Which score would you give this sentence? Why? Pretend you are the student who wrote this essay. What questions or comments would you have for me in a writing conference? Write at least one question and one comment on a piece of paper.*

➤ Independent Practice

Distribute "Comparing My Scores" (page 54) and students' copies of "Self-Evaluation: Opinion Essay" and "Teacher Evaluation: Opinion Essay." *Part One of "Comparing My Scores" has a chart that lists the categories from the rubric. Each category describes one feature of an opinion essay. In the second column, write the score you gave yourself for each feature. Then write the scores I gave you in the third column. Draw a star next to any scores that match. In Part Two, you will think about who will read your opinion essay. Circle any people in the box who might be interested in reading your writing. Write the name of someone in each group of people you circled. Then answer the questions. If you have time, share with a classmate.*

➤ Review

Conduct a teacher-student dialogue to provide feedback on the rubric categories, scores, and the similarities and differences between teacher and student scores. Also, discuss possible authentic audiences for student writing.

➤ Closing

You used a chart to review the scores you gave your essay. Then you looked at the scores I gave your writing. You also thought about the best audience for your writing.

Teacher Evaluation: Opinion Essay

Student Name: _____   **Score:** _____

	4	3	2	1
Thesis Statement— Topic	The thesis statement clearly introduces a topic about school clothes.	The thesis statement introduces a topic about school clothes.	The thesis statement introduces a topic.	The introductory paragraph does not have a thesis statement, or it is not about a specific topic.
Thesis Statement— Opinion	The thesis statement clearly states the author's opinion about the same topic.	The thesis statement includes an opinion about the topic of school clothes.	The thesis statement includes an opinion.	The thesis statement does not include an opinion.
Body Paragraphs	Each body paragraph clearly explains one reason that supports the author's opinion about school clothes.	Each body paragraph explains a reason that relates to the author's opinion about school clothes.	Each body paragraph has a reason for the author's opinion.	The essay does not have body paragraphs, or they do not have reasons that support the author's opinion.
Descriptive Words and Details	The body paragraphs have supporting details that include descriptive words.	The body paragraphs have details that describe school clothes.	The body paragraphs have descriptive words.	The body paragraphs do not have descriptive words or details about the topic.
Transition Words	The author uses transition words correctly to clearly connect reasons to his or her opinion about school clothes.	The author uses transition words to connect reasons to his or her opinion about school clothes.	The author uses a few transition words to connect reasons to his or her opinion.	The author does not use transition words to connect reasons to an opinion.
Concluding Paragraph	The essay has a concluding paragraph that directly relates to the topic and restates the author's opinion about school clothes.	The essay has a concluding paragraph that relates to the thesis statement or restates the author's opinion about school clothes.	The essay has a concluding paragraph about the topic or the author's opinion.	The essay does not have a concluding paragraph.
Conventions	The author uses correct spelling, capitalization, and punctuation in the essay.	The author uses correct spelling, capitalization, and punctuation most of the time in the essay.	The author uses some correct spelling, capitalization, and punctuation in the essay.	The author had trouble using correct spelling, capitalization, and punctuation in the essay.

Name(s): _____

Comparing My Scores

➤ Part One

- In the second column, write the score you gave yourself for each category of the rubric.
- Then write the scores the teacher gave you in the third column.
- Draw a star next to any scores that match.

Categories from the Rubric	My Scores	Teacher Scores
The thesis statement introduces a topic about school clothes.		
The thesis statement includes the author's opinion about the same topic.		
Each body paragraph explains one reason that supports the author's opinion about school clothes.		
The body paragraphs have supporting details that include descriptive words.		
Transition words connect reasons to the author's opinion about school clothes.		
The concluding paragraph directly relates to the topic and restates the author's opinion about school clothes.		
The essay has correct spelling, capitalization, and punctuation.		

➤ Part Two

Think about who might be interested in reading your opinion essay. Circle any people in the box below who will be your audience. Write specific names next to any people you circled. Then answer the questions below.

> teachers _____   other people at school _____
>
> friends _____   people in the community _____
>
> family members _____

1. Who will read my writing? (Those people are your *audience*.)

   _____

2. What does my essay need to be polished and ready for an audience?

   _____

   _____

3. Why would this audience be interested in reading my opinion essay?

   _____

   _____

All About Informative/Explanatory Writing

➤ Objective

Students will participate in a class discussion and take notes about the characteristics of an informative paragraph. Then they will use key words in sample paragraphs to identify and share with partners the main components in sample paragraphs.

➤ Introduction

Today you will talk with classmates as we think about what makes a strong informative paragraph. Our topic for this module is weather.

➤ Instruction

Informative writing tells readers about a topic. A strong informative paragraph has a topic sentence that tells what the paragraph will be about. The paragraph has facts and examples to explain the topic. It has clear information about the topic. The facts are grouped together in a way that makes sense. This makes it easier for readers to understand. The concluding sentence sums up the paragraph and restates the main idea.

➤ Guided Practice

Display "Mysterious Fog" (page 56), covering up the Teacher Notes. Distribute pieces of cardstock. *Draw lines to make four sections on your piece of cardstock. Label the boxes* topic, facts, examples, *and* concluding sentence. *Let's read this sample informative paragraph. What is the topic? Write it in the correct box.* Continue to discuss and guide students to complete the grid for the other aspects of an informative paragraph. Display "When the Wind Blows" (page 57), covering up the Teacher Notes. *Turn your piece of cardstock over. Make four new sections with the same labels.* Read the paragraph as a class. *What do you notice about this paragraph? How are the paragraphs the same? How are they different? Which paragraph is stronger? Why?*

➤ Independent Practice

Distribute "Clouds in the Sky" (page 58). *Draw a cloud shape around important words in the passage. Use your notes to take turns telling a partner the topic, facts, any examples, and the concluding sentence in the paragraph. Remember that the concluding sentence says the main idea in a different way.* Distribute "Raindrops" (page 59). *Draw raindrops around key words in the paragraph. Take turns again to tell your partner the topic, facts, any examples, and the concluding sentence in the paragraph.* Distribute "Weather Information" (page 60). *Look at your notes and the information your partner shared. Write words or a phrase to describe each part of the informative paragraphs you read with a partner.*

➤ Review

Review students' responses on "Weather Information." Discuss the similarities and differences between the second set of paragraphs and the factors that contribute to the strength of the stronger example.

➤ Closing

You read sample informative paragraphs. We talked about the features of an informative paragraph, and you talked with a classmate about these features in example paragraphs.

➤ Answers

"Mysterious Fog" (page 56): *topic*—fog; *facts and examples*—limits how far we can see, like a cloud, hovers near the ground, dense and thick and heavy, differences in air and ground temperature; *concluding sentence (restates main idea)*—Fog limits how far we can see, so we don't know what is in the fog.

"When the Wind Blows" (page 57): *topic*—wind blowing; *facts and examples*—fast or slow, in any direction, moving air, changing temperatures; *concluding sentence*—That rushing air is wind.

"Clouds in the Sky" (page 58): *topic*—Different types of clouds help us predict weather; *supporting details*—different colors, some are denser than others, more water leads to more rain, darker clouds will produce rain sooner; *concluding sentence (restates main idea)*—Learning about the colors of clouds helps us learn about the weather!

"Raindrops" (page 59): *topic*—People might not understand what makes it rain; *supporting details*—clouds made of water vapor, air changes temperature, water vapor condenses, more drops form; *concluding sentence*—They fall to the ground as raindrops.

Mysterious Fog

Fog makes it hard to see. Fog is like a cloud. It hovers near the ground. Fog is dense and thick and heavy. We usually see fog when the moist air above the ground is warmer than the ground itself. Sometimes fog moves with the wind. It can also settle in one place. It may form in one area, such as a park. There may not be any fog in another area close by, such as the road. This means the ground temperature in one place is colder than in another place. Fog can

change quickly and move suddenly. People often think of it as mysterious. Fog limits how far we can see, so we don't know what is in the fog.

Teacher Notes

This is a <u>strong</u> informative paragraph for these reasons:

- The topic sentence introduces the topic: fog.
- Information is grouped in a way that makes sense.
- The paragraph has details and examples to explain the topic.
- The concluding sentence restates the main idea.

Grade level: appropriate
Lexile estimate: 530L

When the Wind Blows

Sometimes the wind blows. It blows fast or slow. Wind can blow in any direction. When the wind blows, the air moves. Think of a hot-air balloon as a large area of air. When the air in the balloon warms up, it rises. Air in the atmosphere does the same thing. As air cools, it sinks back to the ground. When air warms and rises, cooler air rushes in fast or slow to take its place. That rushing air is wind.

Teacher Notes

This is a <u>weak</u> informative paragraph for these reasons:

- The paragraph does not have a clear topic sentence.
- The topic is general, not specific.
- Some of the information in the paragraph seems out of order.
- The facts lack details to explain the information.
- The information in the paragraph relates to more than one topic and might be confusing for readers.

> Grade level: below
> Lexile estimate: 400L

Name(s): _____

Clouds in the Sky

Different types of clouds help us predict weather. Clouds can be many different shades of white and gray. White clouds are not very dense. They scatter all the colors of the rainbow. This makes them appear white. Sometimes clouds become dark or gray. This means the cloud is much denser than a white cloud. A dense cloud has more water and ice crystals. Weather forecasters use this knowledge to predict when it will rain. The darker the cloud, the sooner it will rain. The whiter the cloud, the less likely it will rain. Learning about the colors of clouds helps us learn about the weather!

Teacher Notes

Grade level: appropriate
Lexile estimate: 470L

Raindrops

Many people know rain when they see it. But they might not understand what makes it rain. The air

and clouds are mostly made of water vapor. As the air and water warm, they become like steam, only

you cannot see it. It is invisible water. The warm air rises. This is like a hot-air balloon. Higher in the

atmosphere, it cools again. As it cools, the water vapor condenses. It becomes tiny drops of water.

Sometimes the water freezes. This becomes snow. The ice, water, and vapor we see give clouds their

shape. Over time more water forms, and the drops become heavy. They fall to the ground as raindrops.

Teacher Notes

Grade level: below
Lexile estimate: 390L

Name(s): _____

Weather Information

Look at your notes. Think about what your partner said about the paragraph you read. With your partner, write words or a phrase to describe each part of the informative paragraphs you read.

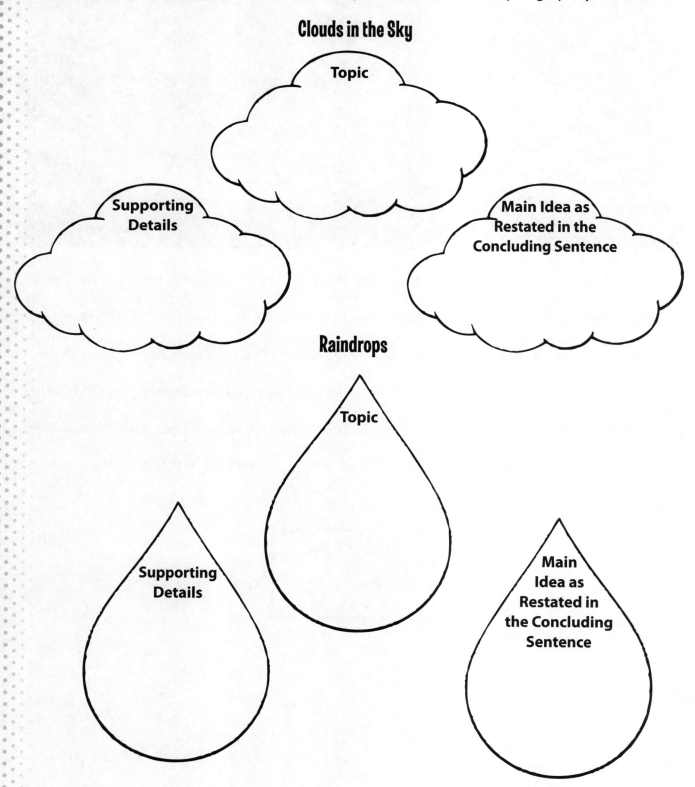

Clouds in the Sky

Topic

Supporting Details

Main Idea as Restated in the Concluding Sentence

Raindrops

Topic

Supporting Details

Main Idea as Restated in the Concluding Sentence

Topic Sentences

➤ Objective

Students will work with partners to read and identify strong and weak topic sentences. They will then practice writing topic sentences and research to gather information for their own informative paragraphs.

➤ Introduction

You will read sample topic sentences with a partner and think about what makes a strong topic sentence. You will also practice writing topic sentences. Then you will choose a topic for your informative paragraph and study to learn more about your topic.

➤ Instruction

The topic sentence tells readers what the paragraph will be about. It states the main idea. Readers can tell what information they will read about in the paragraph. State the topic in an interesting way so readers will want to continue reading the paragraph.

➤ Guided Practice

Distribute "The Best Topic Sentences" (page 62) and yellow and red crayons or pencils. *Work with a partner to read each sentence. Decide which sentences are strong topic sentences. Next to those sentences, color the suns yellow. Next to sentences that are weak topic sentences, color the suns red. With your partner, choose one strong topic sentence. Copy it on the line in Part Two. Discuss what makes it a strong topic sentence. Write your reason. Do the same thing for a weak topic sentence. Then work together to rewrite one of the weak topic sentences as a strong topic sentence.*

➤ Independent Practice

Distribute "Writing Topic Sentences" (page 63). *Look at the pictures in each box in Part One. Think of a topic that might go with each picture and write a topic sentence in each box. Remember, a topic sentence introduces a topic that the informative paragraph will be about. Answer the questions in Part Two to think about a weather topic for your informative paragraph.*

Distribute "Planning Ahead" (page 64). Provide research materials as appropriate for your students. *Read to learn more about your topic. Write a check mark by each study idea you are able to do. (You may not be able to do every idea.) Take notes as you read. Write key words, phrases, and sentences about your topic in the cloud shapes. Then draw arrows to connect ideas that go together.*

➤ Review

Review students' responses to "The Best Topic Sentences" and explain that informative writing includes information that can be proven with facts and other evidence that explain the topic. Encourage students to share their sample topic sentences from this page and also "Writing Topic Sentences."

➤ Closing

You read topic sentences and then practiced writing them. You also decided on a topic for your informative paragraph. Then you read to gather information and ideas about your topic.

➤ Answers

"The Best Topic Sentences" (page 62): strong (yellow) sentences: 2, 3, 4, 5, 6; the other sentences (red) are vague or express an opinion that cannot be proven with fact.

Name(s): _____

The Best Topic Sentences

➤ Part One

Read and discuss the sentences below with a partner.

- Color the sun **yellow** next to any sentence that is a **strong** topic sentence.
- Color the sun **red** next to any sentence that is a **weak** topic sentence.

1. When the sun shines, I have more energy.

2. It takes a lot of snowflakes to cover the ground.

3. People who live in cold places have more than one word to describe snow.

4. There are many different types of rain.

5. Hurricanes, typhoons, and cyclones are the same type of storm.

6. Many places experience very different weather at different times of the year.

7. My brother likes cool, cloudy days.

8. The weather affects people in different ways.

➤ Part Two

1. Choose one strong topic sentence from above. Copy it here. _____

_____

2. Explain why it is a strong topic sentence. _____

_____

3. Choose one weak topic sentence from above. Copy it here. _____

_____

4. Explain why it is a weak topic sentence. _____

_____

5. Rewrite the weak topic sentence to make it a strong topic sentence. _____

_____

Name(s): _____

Writing Topic Sentences

➤ Part One

Look at the pictures in each box. Write a topic sentence about each picture. Remember, a topic sentence introduces a topic that the informative paragraph will be about.

➤ Part Two

Answer the questions below to think about a weather topic for your informative paragraph.

1. What are your favorite topics about weather? _____

   _____

2. What do you find most interesting about weather? _____

   _____

3. What unusual type of weather would you like to learn more about? _____

   _____

4. What weather is most common where you live? How do people who live there describe the weather?

   _____

   _____

   _____

5. Write the topic for your informative paragraph. _____

6. Write a topic sentence for your informative paragraph.

   _____

   _____

Name(s): _____

Planning Ahead

Read to learn more about your topic. As you read, take notes. Write key words, phrases, and sentences about your topic in the cloud shapes. Draw arrows to connect ideas that go together. Make a check mark by each study idea you are able to complete. *Note:* You may not be able to do every idea.

☐ Read a book.

☐ Look at a website.

☐ Listen to an expert (podcast, teacher, guest speaker, etc.)

☐ Talk to people who know about the topic.

☐ Think about my own experiences and background knowledge.

Supporting Details

➤ Objective

Students will work in small groups to complete a K-W-L chart. Then they will brainstorm descriptive weather words and write details and examples to support facts about their chosen topics.

➤ Introduction

Today you will think about what you already know and what you want to learn about your weather topic. You will also brainstorm words that describe your topic. Then you will write facts and examples about the topic of your informative paragraph.

➤ Instruction

Supporting details help readers better understand the topic. This information may include facts, definitions, concrete words, or examples related to the topic. Group details together to help readers better understand the topic. Use exact nouns and action verbs to create a mental picture for your reader. Define any words about your topic that might be new for your readers.

➤ Guided Practice

Distribute "Learning About the Weather" (page 66). *Work with a small group to complete the first two columns of the chart. Think about what you already know about weather and your topic. What do you know about the topics of other members of your group? Share and discuss your ideas and background knowledge. What do you want to know about your topic? What will you need to learn to write an informative paragraph? Write your questions in the second column. Also write ideas of what you would like to learn and study about your topic.* Provide appropriate research materials and resources for students. *Use the third column to take notes as you complete your research.*

➤ Independent Practice

Distribute "Weather Words" (page 67). *Think about words we use to describe different types of weather. Work with a partner to brainstorm words you use or have read or heard to describe each type of weather. Write these words in the appropriate area of the circle. Circle the words that relate to the topic of your informative paragraph.*

Distribute "Supporting My Ideas" (page 68). Refer to your notes on Part Two of "Writing Topic Sentences" (page 63) and "Planning Ahead" (page 64). *Under each umbrella, write one fact about your topic. Then write details or examples about that fact in each umbrella. Share your answers with a partner. Ask and answer questions to make sure your details make sense and are easy for readers to understand.*

➤ Review

Review and introduce additional weather words in a class discussion to assist students as they complete "Weather Words." Model how to write details and examples related to a specific fact, as needed, to assist students in completing "Supporting My Ideas."

➤ Closing

You listed ideas about what to study and learned more about your topic. You also wrote descriptive words, details, and examples to explain facts about your topic.

➤ Answers

"Weather Words" (page 67): Some words are above grade level; introduce and teach as domain-specific words with simple definitions and pictures as needed.
Rain—downpour, drizzle, drought, flood, mist, puddle, rainbow, rainfall, shower, sprinkle
Snow—blizzard, drift, flurries, slush, snowflake, snowstorm
Wind—breeze, gale, gust
Storms—hail, hurricane, lightning, rumble, thunder, tornado
Sun—clear, hot, mild, pleasant, shadows, sunny, sunshine, warm
Other weather-related words—chilly, cold, cool, fog, forecast, freezing, frost, ice, icicle, observe, predict, temperature

Name(s): _____

Learning About the Weather

Work with your small group to complete the first two columns of the chart.

1. Think about what you already know about weather and your topic. What do you know about the topics of other members of your group?

   - Write what you know in the first column of the chart.
   - Share and discuss your ideas and background knowledge.

2. What do you want to know about your topic? What will you need to learn to write an informative paragraph?

   - Write your questions and ideas to study in the second column.

3. Research to learn more about your topic. Use the third column to take notes about what you learn.

K What I **K**now	W What I **W**ant to Know	L What I **L**earned

Weather Words

Think about words we use to describe different types of weather.

Work with a partner to brainstorm words you use or have read or heard to describe each type of weather. Write these words in the appropriate area of the circle.

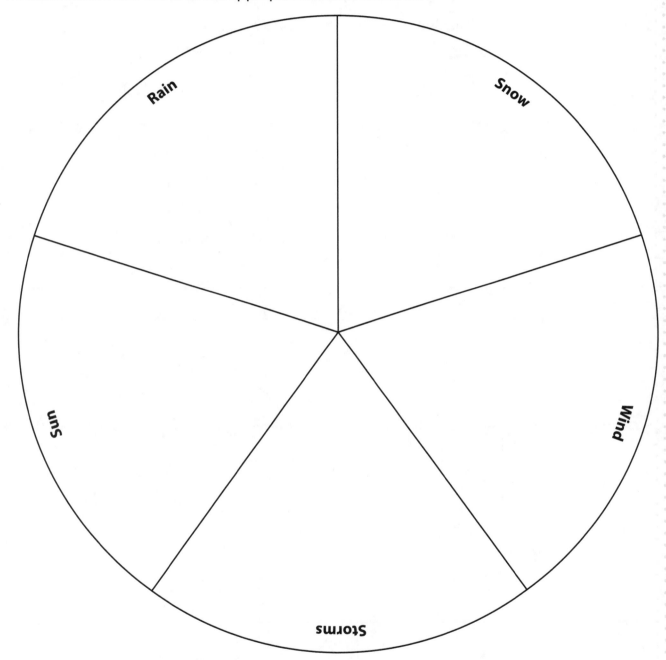

Circle the words that relate to the topic of your informative paragraph.

Name(s): _____

Supporting My Ideas

➤ **Part One**

1. Under each umbrella write one fact about your topic. Refer to your notes on Part Two of "Writing Topic Sentences" (page 63) and "Planning Ahead" (page 64).

2. In each umbrella, write details or examples about that fact.

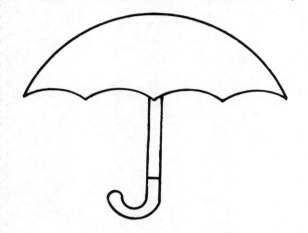

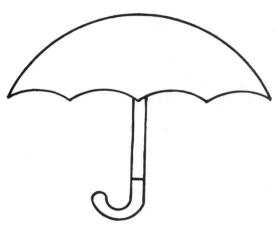

_____   _____

_____   _____

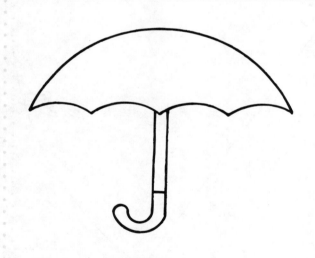

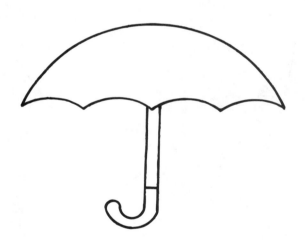

_____   _____

_____   _____

➤ **Part Two**

1. Share your answers with a partner.

2. Ask and answer questions to make sure your details make sense and are easy for readers to understand.

Transition Words

➤ Objective

Students will work with partners to categorize transition words in sample sentences. Then they will practice writing sentences with transition words for their informative paragraphs.

➤ Introduction

You will read sample sentences and notice the transition words. You will think about how these words add meaning to the sentences. Then you will practice writing sentences about your topic with transition words in your sentences.

➤ Instruction

Transition words connect sentences with main ideas to help readers understand an informative paragraph. These words connect ideas in an order that makes sense. Authors use transition words for different reasons. Some transition words introduce a time or place. Discuss examples (when, before, after, later; there, over, near, far). *Transition words can explain information and reasons.* Discuss examples (because, for example, one reason, since, so). *Authors use transition words to add more information about the topic. They may explain how two things are alike or different.* Discuss examples (also, and, another, as, but, too).

➤ Guided Practice

Distribute "Making Sense Out of Information" (page 70). Read the words in the table aloud and remind students these are the roles transition words might fill in a sentence. *Work with a partner to read the sentences in Part One. Notice the underlined transition words. On the line next to each sentence, write the category name for the transition word.*

➤ Independent Practice

Review your ideas and sample sentences from "Planning Ahead" (page 64), "Learning About the Weather" (page 66), and "Supporting My Ideas" (page 68). Circle the words in the chart that you could use in your sentences. Use your notes and ideas to write sentences for your informative paragraph about weather. Write your sentences on a separate piece of paper. Include at least one transition word from the chart in each sentence.

➤ Review

Review with students how they might include transition words in sentences about their chosen weather topic. Invite students to volunteer sample sentences for class discussion.

➤ Closing

You studied transition words and observed how they are used in sentences. You also practiced writing sentences with transition words for your informative paragraph.

➤ Answers

"Making Sense Out of Information" (page 70): 1. alike; 2. more information; 3. location; 4. location; 5. explain; 6. time; 7. more information; 8. time; 9. explain; 10. alike

Making Sense Out of Information

➤ Part One

- Work with a partner to read the sentences. Notice the underlined transition words.
- Look at the lists of transition words below. At the top of each list is a category name. This explains the reason for the transition word.
- On the line next to each sentence, write the category name for that transition word.

_____ 1. Fog is <u>like</u> a cloud.

_____ 2. Fog can <u>also</u> settle in one place.

_____ 3. <u>There</u> may not be fog on the road.

_____ 4. Moist air <u>above</u> the ground is warmer than the ground itself.

_____ 5. Fog limits how far we can see, <u>so</u> we don't know what is in the fog.

_____ 6. <u>When</u> the wind blows, the air moves.

_____ 7. <u>As</u> air cools, it sinks back to the ground.

_____ 8. Dark clouds mean it will rain <u>soon</u>.

_____ 9. The weatherman called it a drought <u>because</u> it had not rained for a long time.

_____ 10. Drops of water become heavy <u>and</u> fall to the ground as raindrops.

Time	Location	Explain/Examples	More Information or Alike/Different
about	above	because	also
after	across	for example	and
at	around	next	another
before	below	one reason	as
finally	between	since	but
later	by	so	like
next	here		too
soon	into		
then	off		
until	there		
when			

➤ Part Two

- Review your ideas and sample sentences from "Planning Ahead" (page 64), "Learning About the Weather" (page 66), and "Supporting My Ideas" (page 68).
- Circle words in the chart above that you could use in your sentences.
- Use your notes and ideas to write sentences for your informative paragraph about weather. Write your sentences on a separate piece of paper.
- Include at least one transition word in each sentence.

Concluding Sentences

➤ Objective

Students will practice summarizing one or more sample paragraphs in a single concluding sentence. Then they will identify key words from notes and writing about their topics, receive input from partners, and draft concluding sentences for their informative paragraphs.

➤ Introduction

You will practice thinking of a concluding sentence for one or more sample paragraphs. Then you will use key words and notes to think about a concluding sentence for your informative paragraph about weather. You will also receive comments from a partner to help you.

➤ Instruction

The concluding sentence of an informative paragraph is about the same topic as the information in the paragraph. It restates the topic sentence in different words. It also summarizes the main idea. A strong concluding sentence gives readers a sense that the paragraph is finished. Your paragraph might explain something or give examples. The concluding sentence should tie it all together.

➤ Guided Practice

Read sample informative paragraphs to students from this module or classroom resources. *As I read this paragraph, listen closely to what the paragraph is about. What information does the author explain? Think about how you would sum up what the paragraph says in one sentence. Then turn and share your single sentence with a partner. Write down your partner's sentence when he or she shares. Read back over your sentences. Which characteristics of a strong concluding sentence did you include?*

➤ Independent Practice

Distribute "Bursting with Information" (page 72) and students' copies of "Writing Topic Sentences" (page 63), "Planning Ahead" (page 64), "Learning About the Weather" (page 66), "Weather Words" (page 67), "Supporting My Ideas" (page 68), and "Making Sense Out of Information" (page 70) as needed. *Look over your notes and practice sentences from activities you have completed during this module. Write the five most important words from your paragraph information in the suns. Trade papers with a partner. Read your partner's words then write a concluding sentence based on what you think his or her paragraph is about. Read the sample concluding sentence your partner wrote on your paper. Write a concluding sentence for your informative paragraph based on your key words and your partner's ideas.*

➤ Review

Review characteristics of a strong concluding sentence: it restates the topic, summarizes the main idea, ties information together, and provides a sense of closure for readers. Review students' responses to the Think-Pair-Share activity in Guided Practice and discuss possible concluding sentences together as a class.

➤ Closing

You practiced thinking of a concluding sentence for sample paragraphs. Then you used key words and ideas from a partner to write a concluding sentence for your informative paragraph.

Name(s): _____

Bursting with Information

➤ Part One

1. Review your notes and practice sentences from activities you have completed during this module.

2. Write the five most important words from your paragraph information in the suns.

➤ Part Two

1. Trade papers with a partner.

2. Read your partner's words then write a concluding sentence based on what you think his or her paragraph is about.

    _____

    _____

    _____

3. Read the sample concluding sentence your partner wrote on your paper.

4. Write a concluding sentence for your informative paragraph based on your key words and the ideas from your partner.

    _____

    _____

    _____

First Draft and Peer Review

➤ Objective

Students will write first drafts of their informative paragraphs, then they will participate in a peer-review activity.

➤ Introduction

Today you will write a first draft of your informative paragraph about weather. Then you will work with a partner to give and receive comments about your writing.

➤ Instruction

When you write the first draft, you write sentences about all your ideas. This is when you start to bring together your thoughts and notes about your topic. As you write, you may find you need more information about something you want to say. In a first draft, it is okay to cross out words. You can write notes along the sides of your paper about changes you would like to make. First drafts are also called rough drafts: they are messy, and that's okay.

➤ Guided Practice

Guide students through writing their first drafts. *Write your topic sentence from "Writing Topic Sentences" (page 63). Look at your notes from "Planning Ahead" (page 64). Then write one or more sentences for each idea in your informative paragraph. Now look at your notes and writing from "Learning About the Weather" (page 66), "Weather Words" (page 67), "Supporting My Ideas" (page 68), and "Making Sense Out of Information" (page 70). Add sentences from these pages to your rough draft. Copy your concluding sentence from "Bursting with Information" (page 72).*

After you write your first draft, you will trade papers with a partner. What will you look for when you read a classmate's writing?

Display "Helping Each Other" (page 74) and review parts of an informative paragraph and categories for scoring.

➤ Independent Practice

Distribute "Helping Each Other." Pair students with partners to review students' first drafts of their informative paragraphs. *Read your partner's first draft. Make a check mark or write a comment for each part of your partner's informative paragraph in the column that best describes his or her writing. Then complete the sentence frames to help your partner understand your comments. Think about how your partner showed strong informative writing in his or her paragraph. Then suggest ways he or she could make the paragraph more interesting for readers. The comments from your partner will give you ideas about how you can strengthen your writing. You make the final decision on what you change in your writing.*

➤ Review

Discuss the impact revising has on the writing process. Review specific parts of informative writing listed on the chart, as needed, to guide students as they write their first drafts. Think aloud about how to score a sample paragraph, for example, one of the paragraphs from Day 1, using "Helping Each Other."

➤ Closing

You used notes and writing from completed activities in this module to write a first draft of your informative paragraph. Then you used a simple rubric and wrote sentences to provide feedback to your partner about his or her writing.

Name(s): _____

Helping Each Other

➤ Part One

1. Trade papers with a classmate.

2. Read your classmate's writing.

3. Make a check mark or write a comment for each part of your partner's informative paragraph.

	Expert	Very Good	Still Learning
Topic Sentence			
Organization			
Details			
Transition Words			
Concluding Sentence			
Conventions			

➤ Part Two

Complete the sentence frames to give your partner feedback about his or her writing.

1. You are an expert at _____ because _____

_____.

2. I liked your _____ because _____

_____.

3. You could try _____ to strengthen your _____

_____.

4. I would like to help you with _____ because

_____.

5. I would like you to help me with _____ because

_____.

Second Draft and Self-Evaluation

➤ Objective

Students will think about qualities of informative writing. They will evaluate and revise their writing using a rubric and classmates' comments.

➤ Introduction

Before today, you did a peer-review activity with a classmate. Today you will reread those comments. You will also use a rubric. The comments and rubric will help you make changes and write a second draft of your paragraph.

➤ Instruction

It is important to look closely at our writing. We can ask questions to help make our writing better. We can also use a rubric. A rubric is a learning tool. It highlights specific parts of writing. A rubric outlines strong and weak writing. For example, the rubric we are going to look at talks about topic sentences. The rubric describes strong topic sentences. It also describes weak topic sentences. Which one do you want in your paragraph? (a strong topic sentence) Today we're going to use a rubric to make our writing better.

➤ Guided Practice

Distribute "Self-Evaluation: Informative Paragraph" (page 76). Introduce the rubric categories on the self-evaluation. *We've already talked about topic sentences. Let's look at the last row. What are conventions?* (grammar, word usage, capitalization, punctuation, and spelling) *Why are these things important?* (Without them, writing can be unclear and hard to read.) *We want our writing to have a clear meaning. We want readers to understand what we are saying. So, strong conventions are important.*

What does a score of 4 in conventions mean? (The sentences are complete, and there are very few errors in grammar, word usage, capitalization, punctuation, and spelling.) *What does a score of 1 in conventions mean?* (The sentences are incomplete. There are many errors in grammar, word usage, capitalization, punctuation, or spelling that make the writing hard to read and understand.) *Do you want to score a 4 or a 1?* (a 4)

Read your paragraph. Compare it to the rubric. Now that you have this rubric, what do you want to do? (change the paragraph so it earns a 4 in each category)

➤ Independent Practice

Look at your notes from "Helping Each Other" (page 74). Reread the comments your classmate gave to you. Was it helpful to have someone else read your writing? Did your classmate make you want to change something? Did this change make your writing stronger? Do you think other readers will like this change? Discuss.

Use the comments and rubric to write a second draft of your informative paragraph. Ask a classmate for help. Did you use your conventions the right way? Ask him or her, "Are you strong in a specific area (like transition words)?" If so, help a classmate who is having a hard time with this. Then score your second draft using the rubric.

➤ Review

Discuss the impact revising has on the writing process. Review individual categories of the rubric, as needed, to guide students as they write their second drafts.

➤ Closing

Today you made your writing better by looking at a rubric. You also reread comments about your first draft from an earlier lesson. The rubric and the comments helped you write a stronger second draft.

Self-Evaluation: Informative Paragraph

Name: _____   Score: _____

	4	3	2	1
Topic Sentence	My paragraph has a topic sentence that clearly introduces a topic about weather in an interesting way.	My paragraph has a clear topic sentence about weather.	My paragraph has a sentence that mentions weather.	My paragraph does not have a topic sentence that introduces a topic.
Organization	Related information and ideas are grouped together in a way that makes sense to explain the topic.	Related information is grouped together in a way that makes sense.	Some information and ideas are grouped together.	Information and ideas are not grouped together in a way that makes sense.
Details	My paragraph has facts, definitions, and examples that clearly develop my topic about weather.	My paragraph has facts, definitions, details, and examples about weather.	My paragraph has some details, such as facts, definitions, or examples about weather.	My paragraph does not have many details about weather.
Transition Words	I use a variety of transition words to connect my sentences and ideas back to the main idea of my paragraph.	I use transition words to connect ideas within my paragraph.	I use at least one transition word to connect ideas within my paragraph.	I do not use any transition words to connect ideas.
Concluding Sentence	My paragraph has a concluding sentence that summarizes the information or restates my main idea about weather.	My paragraph has a concluding sentence that closely relates to my main idea about weather.	My paragraph has a concluding sentence that is about weather.	My paragraph does not have a clear concluding sentence, or the concluding sentence is not about weather.
Conventions	My sentences are complete, and they have very few errors in grammar, word usage, capitalization, punctuation, and spelling.	Most of my sentences are complete. Any errors in grammar, word usage, capitalization, punctuation, or spelling do not affect the meaning of my writing.	Some of my sentences are incomplete. There are errors in grammar, word usage, capitalization, punctuation, or spelling that make my writing hard to read and understand.	Many of my sentences are incomplete. There are many errors in grammar, word usage, capitalization, punctuation, or spelling that make my writing hard to read and understand.

Final Draft

➤ Objective

Students will work with partners to brainstorm ideas for final drafts. They will think about how to publish their writing for specific audiences. They will then write and illustrate final drafts of their informative paragraphs.

➤ Introduction

You will brainstorm ideas for a handout others can read. It will have information from your informative paragraph and pictures. You will think about who would like to read your handout. Before today, you used a rubric to look closely at your writing. Today you will look at the notes you wrote on your second draft. You will make changes to your informative paragraph and write a final draft.

➤ Instruction

A final draft is as correct as possible. Capital letters are used correctly, and sentences have correct punctuation. Words are spelled correctly. Sentences have correct grammar. Sometimes informative text has pictures to help readers understand the information. Will readers be able to understand the information in your paragraph? Reread your writing to make sure it is organized in a way that makes sense. Who will read your paragraph? Write your final draft with your audience in mind.

➤ Guided Practice

Distribute "Weather Report" (page 78). *When authors publish their writing, they print or send a copy (by hand or computer) for someone else to read. How will you publish your informative paragraph? Talk with a partner about ideas for publishing your final draft. Think about the people who would want to read your informative paragraph about weather. These people will be your audience. Then brainstorm ideas for a handout your audience will read.*

➤ Independent Practice

Distribute students' copies of "Self-Evaluation: Informative Paragraph" (page 76). *Before an audience reads your writing, you will write a final draft. This is where you make your writing the best it can be. Look over the scores you gave your writing. Circle one or two areas you would like to work on to make your writing stronger. Check your writing also for correct conventions. How can you publish your writing?* (type your paragraph, have a classmate help type, ask a teacher or other grown-up for typing help, or copy your paragraph neatly and use a scanner to create a digital copy for publication).

➤ Review

Review categories from the rubric and help students use their notes from "Self-Evaluation: Informative Paragraph," particularly to correct conventions, as they write their final drafts.

➤ Closing

You worked with a partner to plan how to publish your informative paragraph. You also thought about your audience. You looked back at the scores you gave yourself on a rubric. Then you made changes to your writing and wrote a final draft of your informative paragraph.

Weather Report

Work with a partner to brainstorm ideas for a handout. Your handout will have information from your informative paragraph.

My handout will be about:

☐ rain   ☐ snow   ☐ fog   ☐ other: _____

☐ sunshine   ☐ wind   ☐ storms

The title will be: _____

I will add these pictures:

_____

_____

I will decorate my writing with:

☐ a border

☐ different types of lines or boxes

☐ fancy letters

I think these people will want to see my final copy:

_____

_____

In the box below, draw a picture to show what your handout will look like.

Final Evaluation

➤ Objective

Students will compare the scores from their self-evaluations with scores they received from the teacher for their informative paragraphs. Then they will discuss with classmates their responses to the scores they received and complete reflective prompts.

➤ Introduction

Before today, you used a rubric to look closely at your writing. You gave yourself scores for each part of your informative paragraph. Today you will see the scores I gave the final draft of your informative paragraph about weather. I used a rubric like the one you used. You will compare your scores with the scores you receive from me. Then you will think about which scores you most agree with or disagree with and why. You will discuss your thoughts with a partner and write a journal entry.

➤ Instruction

You have already used a rubric to score your informative paragraphs. We use rubrics as a learning tool. They help us think about how we can improve our writing in certain areas. The informative paragraph rubric describes qualities that make strong informative writing. How would you describe informative writing in one sentence? (It gives information about a topic and presents ideas and information clearly.)

➤ Guided Practice

Distribute students' copies of their second drafts along with "Self-Evaluation: Informative Paragraph" (page 76), "What's the Difference?" (page 81), and crayons or colored pencils. *Look at the chart in Part One of "What's the Difference?" What score did you give yourself for the topic sentence? Color the appropriate bar to show that score. Continue for each of the other parts of your informative paragraph.* Distribute students' copies of their final drafts with attached teacher evaluations ("Teacher Evaluation: Informative Paragraph" [page 80]). *Then look at the teacher evaluation. What scores did you receive on your final draft? Color bars in Part Two to show your scores for each part of your informative paragraph. How are your scores different? How are they similar? Which scores do you agree with? Why? Which scores do you disagree with? Why? Write your thoughts in the labeled spaces.*

➤ Independent Practice

Talk about your responses to the prompts on "What's the Difference?" with a classmate. Then write a journal entry. Describe what you have learned from using a rubric. How has receiving comments from classmates and scores from the teacher helped you? How will you use what you have learned to make your writing better?

➤ Review

Review specific categories of the "Teacher Evaluation: Informative Paragraph" rubric with students. Clarify and answer questions about students' scores as needed. Consider having a class discussion about why scores differ.

➤ Closing

You looked back at the scores you gave your writing on a rubric. Then you saw the scores I gave your final draft using a similar rubric. You compared the two sets of scores. You responded to prompts about which scores you agree or disagree with and why. You talked with a partner and wrote a journal entry about what you learned from this activity.

Teacher Evaluation: Informative Paragraph

Student Name: _____   **Score:** _____

	4	**3**	**2**	**1**
Topic Sentence	The paragraph has a topic sentence that clearly introduces a topic about weather in an interesting way.	The paragraph has a clear topic sentence about weather.	The paragraph has a sentence that mentions weather.	The paragraph does not have a topic sentence that introduces a topic.
Organization	Related information and ideas are grouped together in a way that makes sense to explain the topic.	Related information is grouped together in a way that makes sense.	Some information and ideas are grouped together.	Information and ideas are not grouped together in a way that makes sense.
Details	The paragraph has facts, definitions, and examples that clearly develop the author's topic about weather.	The paragraph has facts, definitions, details, and examples about weather.	The paragraph has some details, such as facts, definitions, or examples about weather.	The paragraph does not have many details about weather.
Transition Words	The author uses a variety of transition words to connect his or her sentences and ideas back to the main idea of the paragraph.	The author uses transition words to connect ideas within the paragraph.	The author uses at least one transition word to connect ideas within the paragraph.	The author does not use any transition words to connect ideas.
Concluding Sentence	The paragraph has a concluding sentence that summarizes the information or restates the main idea about weather.	The paragraph has a concluding sentence that closely relates to the main idea about weather.	The paragraph has a concluding sentence that is about weather.	The paragraph does not have a clear concluding sentence, or the concluding sentence is not about weather.
Conventions	The sentences are complete, and the writing has very few errors in grammar, word usage, capitalization, punctuation, and spelling.	Most of the sentences are complete. Any errors in grammar, word usage, capitalization, punctuation, or spelling do not affect the meaning of the writing.	Some of the sentences are incomplete. There are errors in grammar, word usage, capitalization, punctuation, or spelling that make the writing hard to read and understand.	Many of the sentences are incomplete. There are many errors in grammar, word usage, capitalization, punctuation, or spelling that make the writing hard to read and understand.

Name(s): _____

What's the Difference?

➤ Part One

Look at the scores you gave your second draft for each part of an informative paragraph.

Color the appropriate bar to show the score for each part of your informative paragraph.

My Scores					
Topic Sentence	Organization	Details	Transition Words	Concluding Sentence	Conventions
4	4	4	4	4	4
3	3	3	3	3	3
2	2	2	2	2	2
1	1	1	1	1	1

➤ Part Two

Look at the scores you received from the teacher on the final draft of your informative paragraph.

Color the appropriate bar to show the score the teacher gave you for each part of your informative paragraph.

Teacher Scores					
Topic Sentence	Organization	Details	Transition Words	Concluding Sentence	Conventions
4	4	4	4	4	4
3	3	3	3	3	3
2	2	2	2	2	2
1	1	1	1	1	1

Compare the scores you gave your writing with the scores you received from the teacher. Write your thoughts in the spaces below.

I agree with my score(s) for _____ because _____

_____

_____.

I disagree with my score(s) for _____ because _____

_____

_____.

Review

➤ Objective

Students will read a sample paragraph with partners and write sentences that demonstrate each part of an informative paragraph on a graphic organizer. Then they will answer questions about the paragraph.

➤ Introduction

Today you will read a sample informative paragraph. You will work with a partner to think about the parts of the paragraph. You will write sentences from the paragraph on a graphic organizer in a way that makes sense. Then you will answer questions about what you read.

➤ Instruction

We have been learning about informative writing. You have also written an informative paragraph. What is the purpose of informative writing? (It gives information about a topic and presents ideas and information clearly.) *We also call this type of writing explanatory writing. The information in the paragraph explains the topic for readers. What are the parts of an informative paragraph?* (topic sentence, facts and details about the topic, information is in an order that makes sense, concluding sentence). *In this lesson, you will read an example of an informative paragraph.*

➤ Guided Practice

Distribute "Snow Day" (page 83) and "Putting the Parts Together" (page 84). *Read the sample paragraph with a partner. Talk about which sentence matches each part of an informative paragraph. Write each sentence in the correct space of the "wall." Write the detail sentences in an order that makes sense.*

➤ Independent Practice

What is the purpose of an informative paragraph? Why do authors write this kind of paragraph? (to tell readers about a topic or explain something) *Think about the paragraph you just read. How would you describe this informative paragraph? Is it strong or weak? Why do you think this? What did you notice about the way the information was organized? What did you learn from reading the paragraph? How well does the paragraph meet the purpose of an informative paragraph? Why do you think this?*

➤ Review

Review the purpose of informative writing. (It tells readers about a topic and conveys ideas and information in an interesting way.)

➤ Closing

You read an example of an informative paragraph. You thought about how the paragraph shows the qualities of informative writing. Then you worked with a partner to write sentences from the paragraph on a graphic organizer. You also answered questions about the paragraph.

➤ Answers

"Snow Day" (page 83): *topic sentence*—When dark clouds hang low in the sky and the air feels cold, it might be the right weather for snow; *facts and details/other information*—any sentences within the body of the paragraph; *concluding sentence*—Every time the weather is just right, it snows.

Snow Day

When dark clouds hang low in the sky and the air feels cold, it might be the right weather for snow. Snow forms when the air temperature is below freezing. There has to be moisture in the air for snow. If the air is too dry, it will not snow. Warmer air holds more water vapor. Sometimes it is below freezing but not extremely cold. Then there is a good chance for snow. It is possible for snow to reach the ground even if the temperature is a little above freezing. The snowflakes begin to melt when they reach the warmer air. If it cools just right, the moisture evaporates a little. This creates cooling. It makes the snowflakes melt slower. When the wind blows, the snow might be denser. Once snow lands on the ground, weather continues to affect it. Snow can start to melt and refreeze again. Over the course of a winter, snowfall builds up in some places. Every time the weather is just right, it snows.

Teacher Notes

Grade level: appropriate
Lexile estimate: 550L

Photograph ©Malcolm Murdoch (*https://www.flickr.com/photos/mildswearwords/3251014897/*), CC BY-SA 2.0.

Name(s): _____

Putting the Parts Together

➤ Part One

- Read "Snow Day" (page 83) with a partner.
- Discuss which sentence matches each part of an informative paragraph.
- Write each sentence in the correct space of the "wall" below.

Topic Sentence	Fact/Detail	Fact/Detail

	Other Information	Concluding Sentence	

➤ Part Two

1. Why did the author write this informative paragraph?

   _____

2. How would you describe this informative paragraph? Why?

   _____

3. What did you notice about the way the information was organized?

   _____

4. What did you learn from reading the paragraph?

   _____

5. How well do you think the paragraph meets the purpose of an informative paragraph? Why?

   _____

Introductory Paragraphs

➤ Objective

Students will participate in a "Give One, Get One" activity. They will use their ideas to write thesis statements and sentences for introductory paragraphs.

➤ Introduction

During this module, you will write an informative essay. An essay is a longer piece of writing. You will trade ideas with classmates to brainstorm about a topic. Then you will choose a topic and think about what you want to say about that topic. You will also write a thesis statement. Then you will plan and write sentences for the first paragraph of your essay. Our topic for this module is how money changes over time.

➤ Instruction

The first paragraph in an informative essay is called an introductory paragraph. This first paragraph has a thesis statement. A thesis statement is a sentence that tells readers the topic of the essay. Another way to think of this is that the thesis statement presents the main idea of the essay. The introductory paragraph helps readers know the information that will be in the body of the essay. Once you choose a topic and write a few sentences, you will know better which ideas you want to learn more about.

➤ Guided Practice

Display pictures of coin and paper money. *What are some things we could say about money in our country? How has money changed over time?* As a class, brainstorm ideas about the topic. Show students age-appropriate print and online resources, as necessary, to help them think about the topic. Distribute "Trading Information" (page 86). *Answer the questions in Part One. Then write one of your ideas about money in the first box of the left column in Part Two. Now that you've started to think about the topic, trade ideas with classmates. Talk with one or two classmates and get their ideas. Write their ideas in the right column. Now write another idea you have about money in the second box in the left column. Repeat the process one more time to write in the third boxes in each column.* Guide students through the appropriate boxes as needed.

➤ Independent Practice

Model how to narrow the focus of a topic for an informative essay. *Let's practice thinking of a topic. Which main idea could we use from our discussion? How could we write this as a thesis statement?* Distribute "Write an Introductory Paragraph" (page 87). *The topic of your informative essay is the main idea you want to write about. What will your essay be about? What will you say about this topic? Write a complete sentence that states your topic in an interesting way. This is your thesis statement. Write one or two sentences that tell readers what you will explain in your essay.*

➤ Review

Use "Write an Introductory Paragraph" to model and review with students how to write a thesis statement. (What is the topic, and what do I want to say about the topic?)

➤ Closing

You traded ideas with classmates to brainstorm a topic. Then you wrote a thesis statement and a few sentences for your informative essay.

Trading Information

➤ Part One

Answer the following questions.

1. What do you know about money?

_____

_____

2. What ideas do you have about money?

_____

_____

3. How do you think money has changed over time?

_____

_____

➤ Part Two

1. Write one of your ideas about money in the first box of the left column.

2. Then talk with one or two classmates and get their ideas. Write their ideas in the right column.

3. Think about what you heard from classmates. Write another idea you have about money in the second box in the left column.

4. Talk to one or two different classmates and get their ideas. Write their ideas in the second box of the right column.

5. Continue the pattern with the last row.

Question: How do you think money has changed over time?	
Give One	**Get One**

Name(s): _____

Write an Introductory Paragraph

The topic of your informative essay is the main idea you want to write about.

What will your essay be about?

My Topic

What will you say about this topic? Write one idea in each circle.

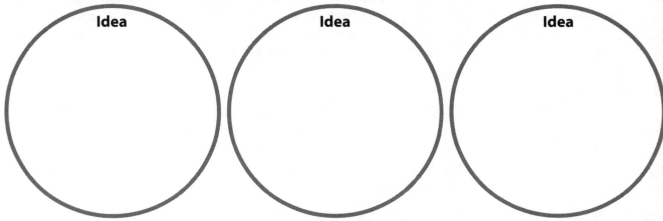

Idea   Idea   Idea

Write a complete sentence that states your topic in an interesting way. This is your thesis statement.

Thesis Statement

Write one or two sentences to let readers know what information you will explain in your essay.

_____

_____

_____

_____

Body Paragraphs

➤ Objective

Students will describe one or more objects related to their topics and practice writing sentences with transition words about their topics. They will also research and take notes to gather information and details about their topics.

➤ Introduction

You will observe objects that have something to do with your topic. Then you will write sentences to describe the objects using sensory details. You will practice using transition words in your sentences. You will also read to learn more about your topic.

➤ Instruction

Body paragraphs form the main part of your essay. They are the paragraphs after the introductory paragraph and before the concluding paragraph. The introductory paragraph tells readers the main points that will be in the essay. There will be one paragraph for each main point of your essay. Each body paragraph is a complete paragraph. Each paragraph will have a topic sentence. It will have facts and details about the main idea in the paragraph. Each paragraph will have a concluding sentence. We arrange the body paragraphs in an order that makes sense.

➤ Guided Practice

Distribute "Describing the Topic" (page 89). Display examples of currency, such as paper money and coins (play money or a small amount of actual money). Show one item at a time. *How would you describe this object? What does it look like? How does it sound when it touches other things? What does it smell like? How does it feel?* Work together as a class to create a word wall on chart paper, poster board, or the whiteboard. Display for student reference as they work on their informative essays.

Now think about your topic. What will you say about the topic in your essay? What is one object you will describe? Use words from our class list to help you describe an object you might write about in your essay.

Distribute "An Organized Essay" (page 90). *Look at how you described the objects on "Describing the Topic." Write two sentences about each object. Use at least one transition word in each sentence. Use the word box on the page to help you. Then trade papers with a partner. Circle the transition words or phrases your partner used in his or her sentences. Talk with a partner about using transition words. How easy was it to use transition words in your writing? What made it easy or hard? How did transition words help you understand the sentences your classmate wrote?*

➤ Independent Practice

Provide appropriate reference materials for students to learn about different forms of money over time. Distribute "Facts and Details" (page 91). *Look at the idea boxes on this page. Write one idea from "Write an Introductory Paragraph" (page 87) in each box. Read books and articles to learn more about your topic. Write facts and details you can use in your essay in the boxes.*

➤ Review

Review appropriate transition words for informative writing and provide sample sentences as necessary. Assist students with researching to gather facts and details about their topics.

➤ Closing

Today you used sensory words to describe your topic. You also learned more about your topic. Then you added facts and details to your notes. You wrote sentences with transition words about the objects you described.

Name(s): _____

Describing the Topic

How would you describe the first object you saw? Think about how it looks, sounds (when it touches other objects), smells, and feels. Write words to describe the object in the boxes below.

Object: _____

Sight	Sound	Smell	Touch

Think of another object that has something to do with your topic. Describe it in the same way.

Object: _____

Sight	Sound	Smell	Touch

Think about your topic.

What will you say about the topic in your essay? _____

_____

_____

_____

What is one object you will describe? _____

An Organized Essay

➤ Part One

- Look at how you described objects on "Describing the Topic" (page 89).
- Write two sentences about each object.
- Include at least one transition word or phrase in each sentence. Use the word box below to help you.

also	finally	for	for example	last	next	second

Object #1

_____

_____

_____

Object #2

_____

_____

_____

➤ Part Two

- Trade papers with a partner.
- Circle the transition words or phrases your partner used in his or her sentences. Look at the words in the box above for ideas.
- Answer the following questions:

1. How easy was it to use transition words in your writing? What made it easy or hard?

_____

_____

_____

2. How did transition words help you understand the sentences your classmate wrote?

_____

_____

_____

Name(s): _____

Facts and Details

In each idea box, write one idea from "Write an Introductory Paragraph" (page 87). Read books and articles to learn more about your topic. Then write facts and details you can use in your essay in the boxes.

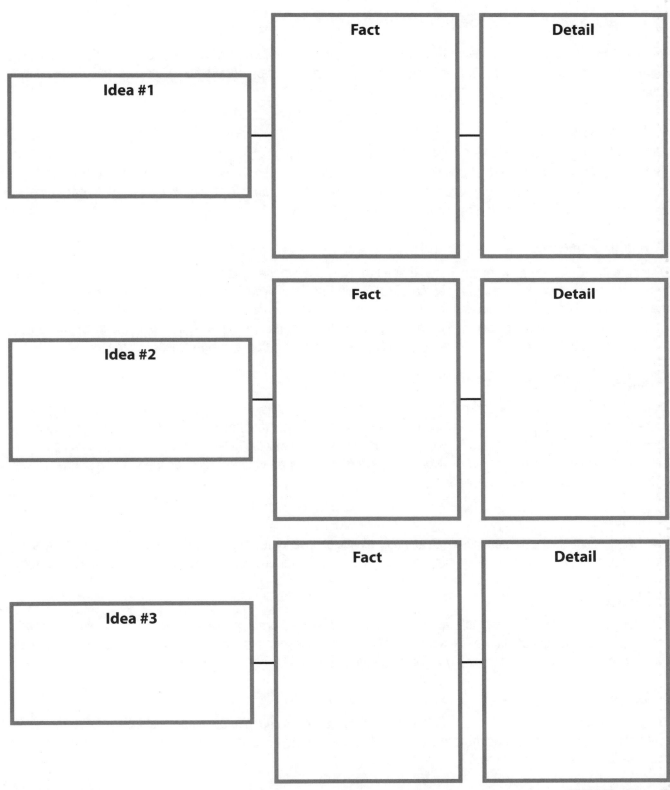

Idea #1   **Fact**   **Detail**

Idea #2   **Fact**   **Detail**

Idea #3   **Fact**   **Detail**

Concluding Paragraphs

➤ Objective

Students will participate in a shared-writing activity in small groups. They will practice writing concluding paragraphs based on the writing generated with classmates. Then they will think about the work they have done so far on their informative essays, practice writing concluding paragraphs, and discuss their writing with partners.

➤ Introduction

You will work with a group to answer questions about a sample informative essay. Then you will write a concluding paragraph for the sample essay. You will practice writing a concluding paragraph for your essay and discuss it with a partner.

➤ Instruction

The concluding paragraph in an informative essay summarizes the main points. We summarize information when we tell it again with fewer words. A concluding paragraph has a topic sentence. It restates your thesis statement in a different way. The concluding paragraph summarizes what the author explained in the essay. A concluding sentence in the paragraph says why the topic is important.

➤ Guided Practice

Distribute "My Conclusions from the Facts" (page 93). *How does money change over time? Work with your small group to read the sample essay. Answer the questions in Part One. What is the topic of the essay? What are the main ideas? For Part Two, work together as a group to write a concluding paragraph for the sample essay. Create your shared-writing piece on chart paper, a computer, or notebook paper. Think about the main idea and information about the topic. Share your group's sample concluding paragraph with other classmates.*

➤ Independent Practice

Distribute "My Concluding Paragraph" (page 94). *Think about the facts, details, and other information you have gathered about your topic. You have written sentences about objects that have something to do with your topic. By now, you also have other notes for your informative essay. Answer the questions and then write a sample concluding paragraph. Think about the work you have done so far on your essay. Then meet with a partner to ask and answer questions about your writing.*

➤ Review

Review with students the different purposes an audience might have for reading their informative essays (to learn about topics of interest, to learn something they need to know, to discover new ideas, and to have questions answered).

➤ Closing

You took part in a shared-writing activity with classmates. Then you practiced writing a concluding paragraph with your group. You thought about the ideas and details you have for your informative essay. Then you wrote a sample concluding paragraph for your essay. You talked about your concluding paragraph with a partner.

➤ Answers

"My Conclusions from the Facts" (page 93): topic—*How money has changed over time*; main ideas—*people traded items of value, not all things had the same value in different communities, today people use coins and paper money because they have the same value from one town to the next*

Name(s): _____

My Conclusions from the Facts

➤ Part One

Read the sample essay. Then answer the following questions.

What is the topic? _____

What are the main ideas in the essay? Work with your group to list them by the bullets.

- _____

- _____

- _____

People use money to trade for things they want. Money is what one person gives someone else in exchange for something of value. Over time, what people use for money has changed.

Years ago, people traded things of value to someone else for something they wanted. Some people used shells. Other people used beads. Certain colors had more value than other colors.

People began to trade outside their community. People from other places had different ways of trading. The shells that had value in one place might not be worth anything in another place. People needed a common type of money that had value to everyone.

Today we say coins and paper money have value. Each type of money is worth a different amount. We use coins to buy things that are worth different amounts of money. People can use money at different stores and places. It has the same value from one town to the next.

> **Teacher Notes**
>
> Grade level: appropriate
> Lexile estimate: 530L

➤ Part Two

1. Create your group-writing piece on chart paper, a computer, or notebook paper.

2. Work together as a group to write a concluding paragraph for the sample essay in Part One. Think about the main idea and information about the topic.

3. Share your group's sample concluding paragraph with other classmates.

Name(s): _____

My Concluding Paragraph

➤ Part One

Think about the work you have done on your essay so far. What facts and details have you learned about the topic for this module?

_____

_____

How did thinking about what you have learned help you write a concluding paragraph for your group piece on "My Conclusions from the Facts" (page 93)?

_____

_____

Now answer the following questions about your writing.

1. What is the main idea of your essay? _____

    _____

2. Why will people want to read your informative essay about changing money? _____

    _____

Think about the three main points you will discuss in your essay.

- • _____

- • _____

- • _____

On a separate piece of paper, write a sample concluding paragraph to summarize these points. Before you write your concluding sentence, reread your thesis statement from "Write an Introductory Paragraph" (page 87).

➤ Part Two

Trade papers with a partner. Read your partner's concluding paragraph. Then complete the sentence frames about your partner's concluding paragraph.

1. From your concluding sentence, I could tell the topic of your essay is _____

    _____.

2. I could tell from your concluding paragraph that your essay will talk about these ideas:

- • _____

- • _____

- • _____

3. In your concluding paragraph, you might try _____

    _____.

First Draft and Peer Review

➤ Objective

Students will write first drafts of their informative essays and participate in a peer-review activity to give and receive feedback on their writing.

➤ Introduction

You have written notes and sample sentences about how money changes. Today you will write a first draft of your informative essay. Then you will talk about your writing with a classmate. You will also write notes about changes you want to make to strengthen your writing.

➤ Instruction

When you write your first draft, you put together all your notes and ideas from what you have learned about your topic. Look back at the topic and main ideas you brainstormed on "Write an Introductory Paragraph" (page 87) to write an introductory paragraph. Make sure your paragraph has a thesis statement. It should also say the main points you will talk about in your essay. Next, you will write body paragraphs. Use the descriptive words and your sample sentences from "Describing the Topic" (page 89) and "An Organized Essay" (page 90). Include information about your topic from your notes on "Facts and Details" (page 91). Add the sample concluding paragraph you wrote on "My Concluding Paragraph" (page 94).

➤ Guided Practice

Guide students through writing their first drafts. Distribute students' copies of "Write an Introductory Paragraph" and scissors. *Cut out the circles on "Write an Introductory Paragraph." In each circle, you wrote one main point of your essay. You will write one body paragraph about each main point. Place the circles in an order that makes sense. Which idea should be first in the essay? Which idea will you write about next? Sometimes the last idea people read about is the one they remember the most. Which point is most important? Decide whether you want that paragraph to be the first body paragraph or the last body paragraph. Then write a first draft of your informative essay. Keep your ideas in order. Start with the introductory paragraph. Write a thesis statement to say what your essay will be about. Write one body paragraph for each main point in your essay. Then add your concluding paragraph.*

➤ Independent Practice

Distribute "Peer Review" (page 96) and various colored pencils. *You will create a color key to check a classmate's first draft for the qualities of informative writing. Choose a color to use to mark each part of your partner's essay. Color the square next to each quality of informative writing to create a color key for your partner. Read your partner's essay. Underline each quality of the essay you notice. Use the colors from your color key. Let's say you colored the box next to the first quality blue. Underline your partner's thesis statement with blue.*

➤ Review

Review the qualities on "Peer Review" and model how to provide verbal feedback, based on what they noticed when they used the checklist, to review a partner's essay.

➤ Closing

You wrote the first draft of your informative essay. You used a color-key checklist to review a partner's essay. Then you shared comments with your partner.

Name(s): _____

Peer Review

➤ Part One

1. Choose a color to mark each part of your partner's essay.

2. Color the square next to each quality of informative writing to create a color key for your partner. Use a different color for each quality.

3. Read your partner's essay. Underline each quality of the essay you notice. Use the colors from your color key.

Informative Writing	Color
The thesis statement says what the essay will be about.	
The introductory paragraph tells readers what information the essay will have.	
Each main point of the essay has its own body paragraph.	
Each body paragraph has a topic sentence, details about the main idea of the paragraph, and a concluding sentence.	
The writing focuses on telling how or why.	
Facts and details explain the topic to readers.	
The essay is organized in a way that makes sense.	
The concluding paragraph summarizes the main points of the essay.	
The closing sentence of the paragraph says why the topic is important.	

➤ Part Two

1. Talk with your partner about what you noticed when you used the color key to check his or her writing.

2. Write one thing you shared with your partner. _____

_____

_____

3. Write one thing you learned from your partner. _____

_____

_____

Second Draft and Self-Evaluation

➤ Objective

Students will use the feedback they received on the peer-review activity to note changes they would like to make to their first drafts, write second drafts, and use a rubric to evaluate their second drafts.

➤ Introduction

Today you will use the feedback you received from the peer-review activity to take notes about things you want to change in the first draft of your informative essay. Then you will write a second draft and use a rubric to edit your second draft.

➤ Instruction

This rubric is similar to the one you used to check your informative paragraph. What have you learned since then about informative writing? Discuss with students. *As you look at the rubric, think about the strengths and weaknesses you notice in your essay. In which areas did you give yourself higher or lower scores? Think about changes you want to make in your second draft. You will decide how you want to improve your writing.*

➤ Guided Practice

Distribute students' copies of "Peer Review" (page 96), along with their first drafts. *Use the feedback you received from a classmate to note changes you would like to make to your first draft. Review the informative writing checklist on page 96 to write a second draft.*

Now let's think about the qualities of informative writing that I will look for when I read your essays. Display "Self-Evaluation: Informative Essay" (page 98). Use a piece of paper to cover all but the first category of the rubric and discuss one category at a time with students. *Place a piece of paper over the second draft of your essay so you see only the first paragraph. Follow along as we talk about what strong writing looks like in this part of your essay. Next to this paragraph, write one thing you would like to change when you write your final draft.* Continue in this manner through the remaining categories on the rubric.

➤ Independent Practice

Distribute highlighters. *Read back through the rubric again, one category at a time. Highlight each quality for the score that best matches that part of your second draft. On a separate piece of paper, write why you gave yourself that score. Make sure you have notes about at least one thing you would like to change in each part of your essay.*

➤ Review

Discuss the impact revising has on the writing process. Review specific categories of the rubric, as needed, to guide students as they edit their second drafts. Discuss the benefits of using a rubric to evaluate writing and reasons for revising a second draft to write a final draft.

➤ Closing

Look at the rubric and think about the strengths and weaknesses of your second draft. Use your notes to write a final draft of your informative essay. We will look at our final copies soon.

Self-Evaluation: Informative Essay

Name: _____   Score: _____

	4	3	2	1
Introductory Paragraph	My essay has an introductory paragraph that introduces a topic about how money changes over time in an interesting way. It has a clear thesis statement.	My essay has an introductory paragraph with a clear thesis statement about money.	My essay has an introductory paragraph that mentions the topic of money.	The topic of my essay is unclear in the introductory paragraph.
Organization	Related information and ideas in my essay are organized in a logical way to make my points about how money changes.	Related information and ideas about how money changes are grouped together in paragraphs.	Some information and ideas about how money changes are grouped together.	Information and ideas about money are not organized in a way that makes sense.
Details	My essay has facts, definitions, concrete details, and examples that clearly develop my topic about how money changes over time.	My essay has facts, definitions, details, and examples about how money changes.	My essay has some details, such as facts, definitions, or examples, about how money changes.	My essay does not have many details about how money changes.
Transitions	I use a variety of transition words to connect ideas about the main point of each paragraph in my essay.	I use transition words to connect ideas within each paragraph of my essay.	I use at least one transition word to connect ideas within my essay.	My essay does not have any transition words to connect ideas.
Concluding Paragraph	My essay has a concluding paragraph that summarizes the information or restates the main idea about how money changes over time.	My essay has a concluding paragraph that closely relates to my main point about how money changes.	My essay has a concluding paragraph that is about how money changes.	My essay does not have a clear concluding paragraph, or the concluding paragraph is not about how money changes.
Conventions	My sentences are complete, and they have very few errors in grammar, word usage, capitalization, punctuation, and spelling.	Most of my sentences are complete. Any errors in grammar, word usage, capitalization, punctuation, or spelling do not affect the meaning of my writing.	Some of my sentences are incomplete. There are some errors in grammar, word usage, capitalization, punctuation, or spelling.	Many of my sentences are incomplete. There are many errors in grammar, word usage, capitalization, punctuation, or spelling.

Review

➤ Objective

Students will review the qualities of effective informative writing with partners and share their ideas with classmates to create a chart. They will then read a sample essay and rate its effectiveness.

➤ Introduction

You will talk with classmates about what makes strong informative writing. Then you will read a sample essay and rate it for how well it meets those qualities.

➤ Instruction

What qualities make a strong informative or explanatory essay? Discuss with the class. *You shared your essay with a classmate and helped each other make changes to strengthen your writing. You also used a rubric to look closely at your writing. These activities summarized the qualities of this type of writing. Today you will read a sample essay. Think about how the author gives readers ideas and information to help them understand the topic.*

➤ Guided Practice

What makes an informative essay interesting and easy for readers to understand? Turn and share one idea with the person on your right. Then turn to the person on your left and share the idea you received from the first classmate you talked with. Invite students at random to share ideas they have received from their classmates. Create a student-generated chart of qualities of informative writing for student reference.

➤ Independent Practice

Distribute "How Money Changes Over Time" (page 100) and "Rate a Sample Essay" (page 101). *Work with a partner to read the sample essay. Look at the chart we created together. Decide how well the sample essay meets the qualities of effective informative writing. Write a phrase or sentence to describe strong writing for each part of an informative essay. Then color a circle on the scale to show how well the sample essay meets each quality.*

➤ Review

Review with students how to evaluate the qualities of the sample essay, as necessary, to rate each category.

➤ Closing

You talked about qualities of informative writing with classmates. Then you read a sample essay. You rated the essay on how well it meets qualities of this type of writing.

Name(s): _____

How Money Changes Over Time

Money changes over time because the pictures honor different people, people use different types of coins, and money needs to stay secure. Our money today looks different than it did many years ago. It has different features than money in the past.

The pictures on money honor different people and places. When this happens, the pictures on money may change. For example, pennies do not look the same. For about fifty years, pennies had a picture of two wheat stalks. People called them wheat pennies. Then pennies had a picture of the Lincoln Memorial. New pennies have a different picture. They have a union shield and a scroll. The first quarters had an eagle on the back. Now the pictures change every few years to show national parks and other sites.

Gold and silver have become more valuable, so different metals are used for coins. The gold and silver coins are not as common. Over one hundred years ago, many people used one-dollar coins. They were made out of silver. People called the coins silver dollars. There are some new coins made out of brass and other metals. Today people use a paper one-dollar bill to buy things. In the past, people also used half-dollar coins. Some people called them fifty-cent pieces. They are no longer made for everyday use.

Paper money changes to make it more difficult to copy. Most paper money used to be green with some white. One-dollar bills are still green. But the other bills have different colors added. Five-dollar bills have purple and gray added. Ten-dollar bills have orange, red, and yellow in the background. Twenty-dollar bills are still mostly green with some peach added. Paper bills have a special thread that glows under ultraviolet light. This makes it harder for people to make fake money.

The government makes changes to money for different reasons. Sometimes a new picture on a coin honors a person or special event in history. Also, we do not need extra coins when other coins or bills will serve the same purpose. Some features keep our money safe from people who want to make fake money. For these reasons, our money will continue to change over time.

Teacher Notes

Grade level: appropriate

Lexile estimate: 540L

Name(s): _____

Rate a Sample Essay

1. Read "How Money Changes Over Time" (page 100) with a partner. Help each other with words and phrases you do not know.

2. Look at the chart you created together with your classmates.

3. On the lines below, write a phrase or sentence to describe strong writing for each part of an informative essay.

4. Then color a circle on the scale to show how well the sample essay meets each quality. *Note:* A score of 4 is strong, while a score of 1 is weak.

Introductory Paragraph

_____

_____

Organization

_____

_____

Body Paragraphs

_____

_____

Details

_____

_____

Concluding Paragraph

_____

_____

Final Evaluation

➤ Objective

Students will review the qualities of effective informative writing as described on a rubric, color squares on a chart to reflect on strengths and weaknesses in their essays, and respond to writing prompts.

➤ Introduction

Today you will work with a small group. You will talk about the qualities of strong informative writing. Then you will look at a rubric. You will compare the scores you gave your informative essay with the scores I gave your essay.

➤ Instruction

You used the "Self-Evaluation: Informative Essay" (page 98) rubric to look closely at your essay. This showed you the qualities I would look for when I scored your essays. You thought about why you gave yourself a certain score. You made notes about how you wanted to strengthen your writing. Today you will compare the scores you gave yourself with those you received from me. Then you will answer writing prompts to think about how you might improve your informative writing.

➤ Guided Practice

Display "Teacher Evaluation: Informative Essay" (page 103). *Which words or phrases on the rubric describe strengths of informative writing?* Divide students into small groups and assign each group a category from the rubric. *Look at the part of the rubric that is your group's focus. Work together to make a list of words that describe strong writing for that part of an informative essay. Then share your list with the class.*

➤ Independent Practice

Distribute students' copies of "Teacher Evaluation: Informative Essay," "Reviewing My Essay" (page 104), and green and blue colored pencils. *In Part One of "Reviewing My Essay," write the number of the score you received for each part of your informative essay. Color the rectangles green that have higher scores (3 or 4). This shows parts of your essay that have strong writing. Color the rectangles blue that have lower scores (1 or 2). This shows parts of your writing you may want to improve and strengthen. Then answer the writing prompts in Part Two.*

➤ Review

Review specific categories of the rubric, as needed, to help students understand the rubric scores. Go over small-group descriptions of effective informative writing and provide examples, as necessary, to help students think of ways they can continue to improve their writing.

➤ Closing

You talked with classmates about the qualities of informative writing. Then you compared the scores you gave your informative essay with the scores I gave your essay. You thought about the strengths of your writing and how you might improve.

➤ Answers

Small-group-work suggested answers: introduce topic in an interesting way, clear thesis statement, organized in a logical way, include concrete details, clear examples, use transition words to connect ideas, concluding paragraph summarizes information, complete sentences, etc.

Teacher Evaluation: Informative Essay

Student Name: _____   **Score:** _____

	4	3	2	1
Introductory Paragraph	The essay has an introductory paragraph that introduces a topic about how money changes over time in an interesting way. It has a clear thesis statement.	The essay has an introductory paragraph with a clear thesis statement about how money changes.	The essay has an introductory paragraph that mentions the topic of money.	The topic of the essay is unclear in the introductory paragraph.
Organization	Related information and ideas in the essay are organized in a logical way to make the author's points about how money changes over time.	Related information and ideas about how money changes are grouped together in paragraphs.	Some information and ideas about how money changes are grouped together.	Information and ideas about money are not organized in a way that makes sense.
Details	The essay has facts, definitions, concrete details, and examples that clearly develop the topic about how money changes over time.	The essay has facts, definitions, details, and examples about how money changes.	The essay has some details, such as facts, definitions, or examples, about how money changes.	The essay does not have many details about how money changes.
Transitions	The author uses a variety of transition words to connect ideas about the main point of each paragraph in the essay.	The author uses transition words to connect ideas within each paragraph of the essay.	The author uses at least one transition word to connect ideas within the essay.	The essay does not have any transition words to connect ideas.
Concluding Paragraph	The essay has a concluding paragraph that summarizes the information or restates the main idea about how money changes over time.	The essay has a concluding paragraph that closely relates to the author's main point about how money changes.	The essay has a concluding paragraph that is about how money changes.	The essay does not have a clear concluding paragraph, or the concluding paragraph is not about how money changes.
Conventions	The sentences are complete, and the writing has very few errors in grammar, word usage, capitalization, punctuation, and spelling.	Most of the sentences are complete. Any errors in grammar, word usage, capitalization, punctuation, or spelling do not affect the meaning of the writing.	Some of the sentences are incomplete. There are errors in grammar, word usage, capitalization, punctuation, or spelling.	Many of the sentences are incomplete. There are many errors in grammar, word usage, capitalization, punctuation, or spelling.

Name(s): _____

Reviewing My Essay

➤ Part One

1. Write the number of the score you received for each part of your informative essay.

	My Score	**Teacher Score**
Introductory Paragraph		
Organization		
Details		
Transitions		
Concluding Paragraph		
Conventions		

2. Color the rectangles that have higher scores (3 or 4) green. This shows the parts of your essay that have strong writing.

3. Color the rectangles that have lower scores (1 or 2) blue. This shows the parts of your writing you may want to improve and strengthen.

➤ Part Two

1. Write a sentence about how the scores you gave your essay compare to the scores you received from the teacher.

_____

_____

_____

2. Write one way your writing shows a quality of informative writing.

_____

_____

_____

3. Describe one way you would like to strengthen your writing.

_____

_____

_____

All About Narrative Writing

➤ Objective

Students will read sample narrative paragraphs and identify qualities of narrative writing. They will observe how actions within an experience happen in a logical order and rewrite a concluding sentence to strengthen it.

➤ Introduction

Today you will learn about qualities of narrative writing. You will read sample narrative paragraphs. Then you will think about how each paragraph shows qualities of narrative writing. A narrative paragraph has a topic sentence, details, actions that happen in an order that makes sense, and a concluding sentence. During this module, your narratives will be about an experience you or someone else had observing an animal in nature.

➤ Instruction

Narrative writing tells about a real or imagined experience. This type of writing uses details that tell about things that happen. The actions involve one or more people, whom we call characters. Narratives often tell an experience that happened to the narrator. The narrator is the person telling the story. Readers may learn a lesson or something new from reading the narrative.

➤ Guided Practice

Display "Amazing Tigers" (page 106, strong example), covering up the Teacher Notes. Distribute "Interesting Narratives" (page 108). Read through the paragraph with students. *Which qualities of narrative writing do you notice in this paragraph? I will read the paragraph again. Listen for the topic sentence. What details do you hear in the story? Do things happen in an order that makes sense? How does the paragraph end? Place a check mark in the first column for each quality you hear.* Distribute "Beaver Dam" (page 107, weak example). Pair students with partners to read the paragraph. *Focus on the second column on this page. Check each quality you notice in the paragraph. Talk about your answers with your partner. Which paragraph is a stronger example of narrative writing? Why? Which paragraph is more interesting to you? Why?*

➤ Independent Practice

Distribute "Bald Eagle Sighting" (page 109) and green and blue colored pencils. *Read the sample narrative paragraph. Highlight the topic sentence green. Circle any words that describe what happens. Circle any words that give details about the five senses. Then highlight the concluding sentence blue.* Distribute "River Walk" (page 110). *Talk with your partner about the order in which things happen in this experience. Write numbers next to the sentences to show the order of the actions. One quality of narrative writing is that the concluding sentence makes sense. It is the natural ending after the things that happen as part of the experience. Choose one of the sample paragraphs you have read in this unit. How could you rewrite the concluding sentence to make it stronger? Write your idea for a different concluding sentence on the lines.*

➤ Review

Review student responses on "Interesting Narratives," checking for understanding.

➤ Closing

You learned about qualities of narrative writing. Then you read sample narrative paragraphs with classmates. You talked about how each paragraph showed qualities of narrative writing.

➤ Answers

"Bald Eagle Sighting" (page 109): *topic sentence*—I stretched my legs out on the dock and gazed at the towering pines on shore; *concrete words and sensory details*—towering pines, soaring, white head and tail feathers, swoop down, giant tree, perched; *concluding sentence*—I jumped into the lake, ready to swim!
"River Walk" (page 110): 1. My family enjoys taking walks along the river; 2. One evening, we saw several rabbits; 3. A small one sat very still as we walked by; 4. It waited until the danger had passed before it hopped into the bushes; 5. A larger bunny nearby was not as fearful; it nibbled the grass as I watched.

Amazing Tigers

Whenever I have the chance to go to the zoo, I head straight for the tigers. They have handsome faces and stripes. I can imagine them using their strength to stalk prey. Once we visited a zoo that had a white tiger. Its fur reminded me of winter snow. The tiger's blue eyes stared right at me. Then it turned its head and prowled through the

bushes in its habitat. I waited to see whether it would find anything to eat. I watched the white tiger for a while. Then I went to the next area that had fiery orange tigers. If I could, I would stay and watch the tigers all day to learn more about these beautiful animals.

Teacher Notes

This example describes a real experience observing an animal and has the following strengths and weaknesses:

- The first sentence introduces "I" (narrator) going to the zoo (situation) to watch the tigers (another character).
- Descriptive words enable readers to picture one of the characters and the events.
- These descriptive words are included: *handsome, stalk, white, winter, stared, prowled, habitat, fiery, orange, beautiful.*
- The paragraph could use more sensory details.
- Action verbs guide readers through events, which are described in a logical order.
- These transition words are included: *Whenever, once, then, if.*
- The concluding sentence flows naturally from the described experience.

Grade level: appropriate
Lexile estimate: 530L

Name(s): _____

Beaver Dam

One time when I was riding in the car, I saw a beaver dam. I knew what it was because it was on a

creek. It was built of sticks. It also had moss and grass. I asked Dad to pull over to the side of the

road so I could get a better view. When I got out of the car, I looked through the trees to try to see

the beavers. They must have been hiding in the dam. It didn't look like their dam made a very big

pond. I would like to go back some time and watch the beavers working on their dam.

Teacher Notes

Grade level: appropriate
Lexile estimate: 510L

Interesting Narratives

➤ Part One

1. Follow along as your teacher reads "Amazing Tigers" (page 106). In the second column of the chart below, check each quality you notice in the paragraph.

2. Read "Beaver Dam" (page 107) with a partner. In the third column, check each quality you notice in the paragraph.

	Amazing Tigers	Beaver Dam
The writing develops a real or imagined experience or event.		
The topic sentence introduces a narrator or characters and a story event or situation.		
The paragraph has concrete words and sensory details to describe the experience or event.		
The actions in the narrative are in a logical order.		
Transition words and phrases guide readers through the actions in the narrative.		
The narrative has a concluding sentence that flows naturally from the narrated experience or event.		

➤ Part Two

Discuss your answers above for each paragraph with your partner. Then answer the following questions:

1. Which paragraph is a stronger example of narrative writing? Why?

   _____

   _____

   _____

   _____

2. Which paragraph is more interesting to you? Why?

   _____

   _____

   _____

   _____

Name(s): _____

Bald Eagle Sighting

1. Read the sample paragraph.

2. Highlight the topic sentence green.

3. Circle any words that give details about what happens. Circle words that tell about the five senses.

4. Then highlight the concluding sentence blue.

I stretched my legs out on the dock and gazed at the towering pines on shore. The lake was still and quiet in the early morning sun. A bird soaring overhead caught my attention. Its white head and tail feathers flashed in the light. A bald eagle! I sat up straighter. Then I turned toward the water to see it up close. I wished it would soar over the lake and swoop down to catch a fish. As I watched, it flew up to a giant tree. It perched at the very top. If anyone was going to get in the water this morning, it would have to be me. I jumped into the lake, ready to swim!

Teacher Notes

Grade level: appropriate
Lexile estimate: 600L

Name(s): _____

River Walk

Read the following narrative and complete the activity below.

My family enjoys taking walks along the river.

Some days we go in the afternoon. Other times,

we go in the evening. I always keep my eyes

open for wildlife. One evening, we saw several

rabbits. They must live in the shrubs along the

path. I knew they were wild because they were

smaller than pet rabbits. A small one sat very still as we walked by. It waited until the danger had

passed before it hopped into the bushes. A larger bunny nearby was not as fearful; it nibbled the grass

as I watched. It's fun to see the rabbits, but I wish we could see unusual animals on our river walks!

1. Discuss with a partner the order in which things happen in this experience.

2. Write numbers next to the sentences to show the order of the actions.

3. One quality of narrative writing is that the concluding sentence makes sense. It is the natural ending after the things that happen as part of the experience. Choose one of the sample paragraphs you have read in this unit. How could you rewrite the concluding sentence to make it stronger? Write your idea for a different concluding sentence on the lines below.

_____

_____

_____

_____

Teacher Notes

Grade level: appropriate
Lexile estimate: 530L

Beginning the Narrative

➤ Objective

Students will brainstorm details about the experiences that will be the topics of their narratives, write topic sentences for their narrative paragraphs, and receive feedback from partners. Then they will brainstorm actions that are part of the experiences and order them in sequence.

➤ Introduction

You will choose an experience to write about in your narrative paragraph. Then you will think about the character(s), setting, and actions that are part of the experience. You will write a topic sentence for your paragraph and number the actions in order.

➤ Instruction

The first sentence of a short narrative piece helps readers understand the experience the author will describe. The writer says who is telling the story. This person is the narrator. There may also be other characters in the narrative. The actions occur in a certain place. We call this the setting. The beginning of a narrative also tells what experience the paragraph will be about. Before you write your narrative, you will want to plan and organize the order of actions in your story. Think about times when you have told someone about something that happened to you. This will help you plan how to describe the experience you will write about. Narratives include details in an order that makes sense. The details help readers understand why the author chose to tell the story.

➤ Guided Practice

Think about an experience you want to write about. What will make this experience interesting for readers? Distribute "Introduce Your Narrative" (page 112). *Who had the experience you will describe? Write notes about the event. List the character(s) and setting that will be part of the narrative.* Distribute "Thinking About Narratives" (page 113). *Use your notes from "Introduce Your Narrative" to complete Part One. Write a topic sentence to tell readers the character(s), setting, and experience you will describe in your narrative.*

Trade papers with a partner to complete Part Two. Read your partner's topic sentence. What experience do you think he or she will write about? Fill in the boxes and return the paper to your classmate. Look at the notes your partner gave you. Then, in Part Three, rewrite your topic sentence.

➤ Independent Practice

Distribute "The Narrative Experience" (page 114). *What happened during the experience you will write about? Write the experience or event in the center circle. In the other circles of the web, write the actions that happened. Make sure to write only things that happened in this experience. Add circles if you need more space to add actions or details. Number the circles outside the center circle to show the order of the things that happened.*

➤ Review

Model writing a sample topic sentence for students and monitor them as they sequence events within their narrative experiences in a logical order.

➤ Closing

You brainstormed ideas for your narrative paragraph. Then you wrote a topic sentence and shared it with a partner. You also planned the order of things that will happen in your narrative.

Name(s): _____

Introduce Your Narrative

1. What experience will you describe?

    _____

    _____

    _____

2. Who had the experience observing the animal? Circle the character who will tell the story. If the experience happened to someone else, write who that person is on the line.

    me   someone else: _____

3. Brainstorm ideas about the narrator or character. What did the narrator do when things happened in the experience? Write words to describe the main character and what he or she did in the box below.

    ```



    ```

4. Where did the experience happen? Write words to describe the setting in the box below.

    ```



    ```

Name(s): _____

Thinking About Narratives

➤ Part One

1. Look at your notes from "Introduce Your Narrative" (page 112).

2. Write a topic sentence to tell readers the character(s), setting, and experience you will describe in your narrative.

_____

_____

_____

➤ Part Two

1. Trade papers with a partner.

2. Read your partner's topic sentence.

3. What do you think his or her narrative will be about? Write your ideas in the boxes below.

Character(s)	Setting

Experience

➤ Part Three

After reading your partner's notes, rewrite your topic sentence.

_____

_____

Name(s): _____

The Narrative Experience

What happened during the experience your narrative will describe?

1. Write the experience or event in the center circle.

2. In the other circles of the web, write the actions that happened. Make sure to write only things that happened in this experience. Add circles if you need more space to add actions or details.

3. Number the circles outside the center circle to show the order of actions that happened.

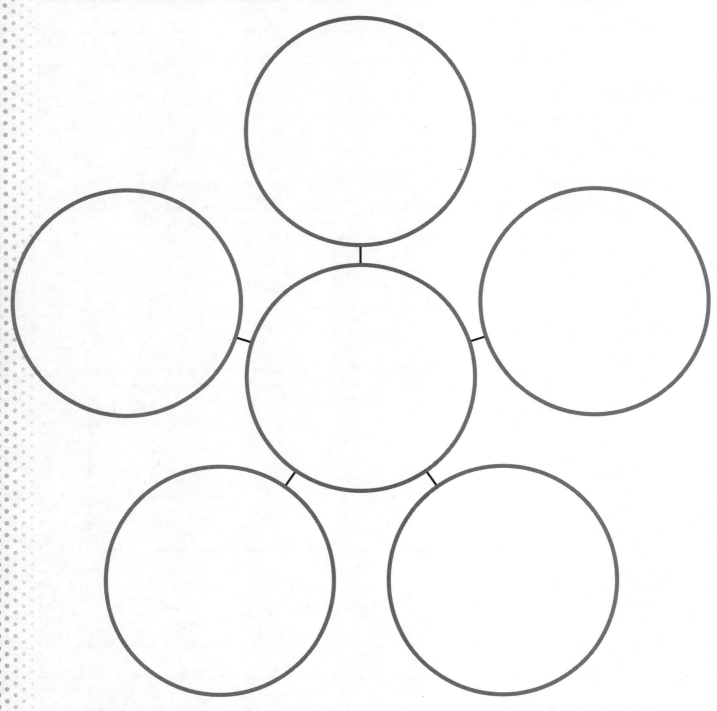

Describing the Experience

➤ Objective

Students will brainstorm sensory details and descriptive words to include in their narrative paragraphs. They will give and receive feedback to make their writing easy for readers to understand and keep their writing interesting at the same time.

➤ Introduction

You will brainstorm details that are about the five senses. The details will be about the topic of your narrative paragraph. Then you will draw a picture of the experience your narrative describes. You will also write sentences that describe the experience.

➤ Instruction

Authors use concrete words and details about the senses to describe actions in a narrative. They describe what characters do when things happen in the story. Details help readers see pictures in their mind about what happens in the narrative. Concrete words help readers understand the actions and setting within a story event.

➤ Guided Practice

Your narrative will be about observing an animal in nature. What senses might a person use in this experience? What detail words can you use to describe what happens? Distribute "The Whole Experience" (page 116). *Think about the topic of your narrative paragraph. Copy your topic sentence or write one sentence to remind you of the experience you will describe in your narrative paragraph. Then write one or more words for each sense in the pie chart.* Invite students to share their descriptive words with the class.

➤ Independent Practice

Distribute "The Perfect Word" (page 117), colored pencils, and highlighters. *Picture in your mind the experience you will describe. Draw the picture in the box. Color the picture to make it more interesting. Then write sentences to describe where the experience takes place. Write sentences about the actions that are part of the experience. Include detail words from "The Whole Experience" and other concrete words to describe your picture. Trade papers with a classmate. Read your partner's sentences and circle any words you don't understand. Highlight words that help you picture the experience your partner will describe in his or her narrative. Use the comments from your partner to rewrite your sentences. Explain your ideas to make your writing interesting and easy for readers to understand.*

➤ Review

Review with students examples of concrete words (nouns, verbs, and adjectives) as well as sensory detail words. Consider creating a class word wall for student reference.

Model how to use sentence context to make concrete words easier for readers to understand while still keeping the writing interesting.

➤ Closing

You brainstormed words to describe the experience in your narrative paragraph. Then you practiced writing sentences with detail words. You also gave and received comments from a classmate to help you make your writing interesting and easy for readers to understand.

Name(s): _____

The Whole Experience

1. Copy your topic sentence or write one sentence that will remind you of the experience you will describe in your narrative paragraph.

   _____

   _____

   _____

2. Write one or more detail words for each sense in the pie chart.

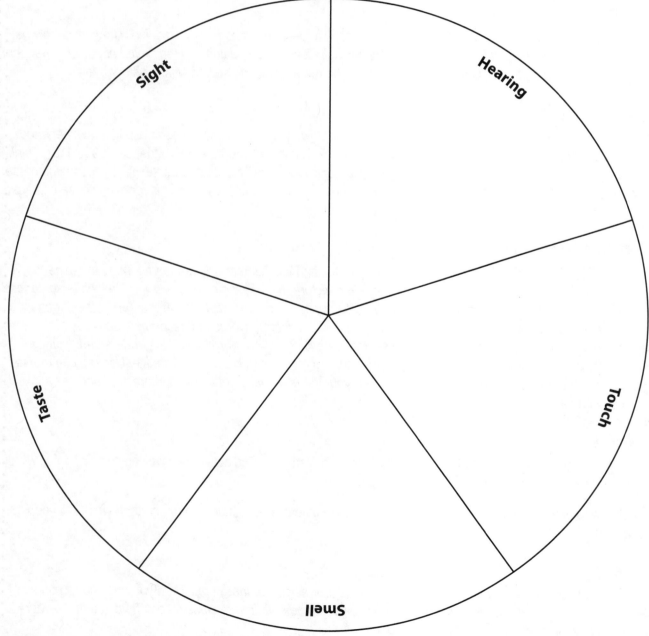

3. Share your descriptive words with classmates.

Name(s): _____

The Perfect Word

1. Picture in your mind the experience you will describe. Draw and color the picture in the box below.

[ ]

2. Write sentences to describe where the experience takes place. Write sentences also about the actions that are part of the experience. Include detail words from "The Whole Experience" (page 116) and other concrete words to describe your picture.

_____

_____

_____

_____

3. Trade papers with a classmate. Read your partner's sentences and circle any words you don't understand. Highlight words that help you picture the experience your partner will describe in his or her narrative.

4. Use the comments from your partner to rewrite your sentences. Explain your ideas to make your writing interesting and easy for readers to understand.

_____

_____

_____

Transition Words

➤ Objective

Students will observe and participate in the placement of transition words within sentences to add meaning and aid in reader comprehension. They will then rewrite sentences they have drafted and include transition words.

➤ Introduction

Today we will notice how transition words add meaning to a narrative paragraph. Then you will practice adding transition words to sentences you have already written.

➤ Instruction

We use transition words to help guide readers through the actions in a narrative event. Not every sentence needs a transition word. The important thing is that the narrative flows in a natural way. In a narrative, transition words give readers a sense of time. The things that happen within an experience are usually described in time order. Transition words connect things that happen to the character(s). They can also connect a character's thoughts with actions.

➤ Guided Practice

Let's read some sample sentences from a narrative paragraph. (Use one of the paragraphs from Module 5: Day 1 or another classroom resource.) *What transition words do you notice in these sentences? How do transition words help you understand what actions happen in the narrative?*

Manipulate transition words (e.g., drag and drop on an interactive whiteboard or move word cards on chart paper) within sample sentences to model and explain how such words clarify meaning and understanding.

➤ Independent Practice

Ensure students have their copies of "The Narrative Experience" (page 114) and "The Perfect Word" (page 117). Distribute copies of "A Path Through the Narrative" (page 119). *Look at the actions you noted on "The Narrative Experience." Which will happen first? Which happens toward the end of the experience? Copy your sentences in order on "A Path Through the Narrative." How can you help readers understand the order in which things happen? How do your character's actions and thoughts connect to each other? Choose transition words from the word box that will help your sentences make sense for readers. Write a transition word that makes sense on the line next to each sentence you copied.*

➤ Review

Review with students how to use transition words. Let them know that transition words do not always need to be at the beginning of a sentence. Provide additional modeling and practice with the whole group using student-generated sentences as time and interest allow.

➤ Closing

You have learned how to use transition words in your narrative writing. These words show the order in which things happen. They help connect characters' actions to thoughts and events.

A Path Through the Narrative

➤ Part One

1. Look at the actions and events you noted on "The Narrative Experience" (page 114). Which will happen first? Which happens toward the end of the experience?

2. Then read the sample descriptive sentences you wrote on "The Perfect Word" (page 117).

3. Copy your sentences in order below. (Note: Leave the short lines before the numbers blank for now.)

_____ ① _____

_____

_____ ② _____

_____

_____ ③ _____

_____

_____ ④ _____

_____

_____ ⑤ _____

_____

_____ ⑥ _____

_____

➤ Part Two

1. Choose transition words from the box below that will help readers understand your sentences. Think about the order in which things happen and how a character's actions and thoughts connect to each other.

after	also	because	before	finally	first
later	next	since	so	soon	then	when

2. Write a transition word that makes sense on the short line next to each sentence you copied.

Concluding Sentences

➤ Objective

Students will read a sample narrative and write strong concluding sentences for the paragraph. Then they will practice writing concluding sentences for their narratives and give and receive feedback from classmates about which concluding sentences are the most effective.

➤ Introduction

You will read an example of a narrative paragraph. Then you will talk with a partner about how to write a strong concluding sentence for the paragraph. You will also practice writing sample concluding sentences for your narrative and share your ideas with a partner.

➤ Instruction

The concluding sentence of a narrative paragraph gives readers a sense of "the end" of the experience. It should make sense after what happened in the narrative. Often the author may look back on why the experience was important. An author may write about what was learned. After you write your narrative, ask yourself, "So what? Why did I choose to write about this experience? Why would readers want to read about it?"

➤ Guided Practice

Distribute "Visiting Relatives and Wildlife" (page 121). *Read the sample paragraph with your partner. Talk about how the narrative ends. How well does the concluding sentence end the paragraph? Why do you think this? How could you rewrite or improve the concluding sentence? Work with your partner to write a new concluding sentence for the narrative paragraph. Share your sentence with the class.*

➤ Independent Practice

Ensure students have their copies of "Thinking About Narratives" (page 113) and "A Path Through the Narrative" (page 119). Distribute "Strong Concluding Sentences" (page 122).

Share your topic sentence and other sentences from your activity pages with a partner.

Listen as your partner says in one sentence what he or she thinks your narrative is about. Trade papers and then answer question three from Part One about your partner's paragraph. Then use your notes, sentences, and your partner's comments to write three sample concluding sentences for your paragraph. Trade papers with your partner. Number his or her concluding sentences for how well they meet the qualities of a strong concluding sentence. Use a "3" for the sentence that ends the paragraph the best and a "1" for the weakest sentence.

➤ Review

Review students' concluding sentences for the sample paragraph and discuss what makes an effective concluding sentence based on the instruction in this lesson. Monitor and assist students as they write their own sample concluding sentences.

➤ Closing

You read an example of a narrative paragraph. Then you worked with a classmate to write a strong concluding sentence. You used your notes and partner's comments to write sample concluding sentences for your own narrative paragraph.

Name(s): _____

Visiting Relatives and Wildlife

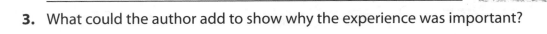

Imagine spending Thanksgiving in the desert. One year, my family went to visit relatives in November. We didn't really have Thanksgiving dinner because we had to drive so many hours to get there. When we got up the next morning, my aunt invited us to play a game. We sat on the patio to play. While we were sitting at the table, I saw a gecko climbing up the concrete wall. It had splotches of green and pink and brown. At first, I almost didn't see it. It blended in with the pink stucco. I watched it sit sideways on the wall without darting away. Maybe it had been around people a lot. After I saw the gecko, I wanted to leave the game and look for other wildlife.

Read the sample paragraph above with a classmate. Talk about how the narrative ends.

1. How well does the concluding sentence end the paragraph? Why do you think this?

   _____

   _____

   In what ways is the concluding sentence strong or weak?

   _____

   _____

2. Why would readers want to read about this experience?

   _____

   _____

3. What could the author add to show why the experience was important?

   _____

   _____

4. How could you rewrite or improve the concluding sentence? _____

   _____

5. Write a new concluding sentence for the paragraph. _____

   _____

6. How did you decide what to say in your concluding sentence? _____

   _____

Teacher Notes

Grade level: appropriate

Lexile estimate: 640L

Name(s): _____

Strong Concluding Sentences

➤ Part One

1. Share your topic sentence and other sentences from "Thinking About Narratives" (page 113) and "A Path Through the Narrative" (page 119) with your partner.

2. Listen as your partner says in one sentence what he or she thinks your narrative is about.

3. Trade papers. Answer the following question about your partner's narrative: Why do you (the reader) think this topic is important and interesting to read about?

_____

_____

_____

➤ Part Two

1. Use your notes, sentences, and your partner's comments to write three sample concluding sentences for your narrative paragraph. (Note: Leave the short lines before the letters blank for now.)

_____   Ⓐ _____

_____

_____

_____   Ⓑ _____

_____

_____

_____   Ⓒ _____

_____

_____

2. Trade papers with a classmate.

3. Number your partner's concluding sentences for how well they meet the qualities of a strong concluding sentence. Use a "3" for the sentence that ends the paragraph the best and a "1" for the weakest sentence. Write numbers on the short lines before the sentences.

First Draft and Peer Review

➤ Objective

Students will write first drafts of their narratives and participate in a peer-review activity to receive feedback on strengths and suggestions for areas that need improvement.

➤ Introduction

Today you will write all of your sentences together in a first draft of your narrative paragraph. You will write the topic sentence. Then you will add the sentences describing the events in your narrative experience. You will also write a concluding sentence to end the first draft of your narrative paragraph. Then you will work with a partner to give and receive feedback about how well your writing and your partner's writing include qualities of narrative writing.

➤ Instruction

A first draft is the first copy we write of the whole paragraph. Often, when we are ready to write a first draft, we already have notes about what we want to include in the narrative. Your first draft will have your topic sentence and other sentences that describe the actions of the narrative experience. It will end with your concluding sentence. You may need to brainstorm additional ideas and details about your topic. Think about the experience of observing an animal in nature that you will describe. If possible, write the experience from your point of view to connect with readers. Use colorful descriptions to help readers take part in the experience.

➤ Guided Practice

Distribute students' copies of "Introduce Your Narrative" (page 112), "Thinking About Narratives" (page 113), "The Narrative Experience" (page 114), "The Whole Experience" (page 116), "The Perfect Word" (page 117), "A Path Through the Narrative" (page 119), and "Strong Concluding Sentences" (page 122). *Look back at your notes from your activity pages. Then write a first draft of your narrative paragraph. Make sure your paragraph describes an experience observing an animal in nature. Write your topic sentence from "Thinking About Narratives." At the end of the paragraph, write your concluding sentence from "Strong Concluding Sentences."*

➤ Independent Practice

Distribute "Peer Review" (page 124) and blue, green, and yellow colored pencils. *Read your partner's first draft. In Part One, write the words that add interest and meaning to the narrative in the box. Then answer the questions. Then in Part Two, read the statements that describe the qualities of narrative writing. Color the box next to each statement to show how well the author wrote that part of his or her narrative paragraph. Use blue to show parts of the narrative that have excellent writing. Use green for parts that meet that quality of narrative writing. Color the box yellow if an area could be strengthened. Write a clear, kind suggestion for any qualities you colored yellow. Look at the words that describe the quality for ideas about how your classmate could strengthen his or her writing.*

➤ Review

Review the qualities of narrative writing as listed on "Peer Review" to check for student understanding before students complete the activity. Discuss sample suggestions students might make about how to strengthen narrative writing.

➤ Closing

You wrote the first draft of your narrative paragraph about observing an animal in nature. Then you took part in a peer-review activity to give and receive suggestions about how to strengthen your narrative writing.

Name(s): _____

Peer Review

➤ Part One

1. Read your partner's first draft.

2. In the box below, write words that add interest and meaning to the narrative.

    ```
    ┌─────────────────────────────────────────────────────────┐
    │                                                         │
    │                                                         │
    │                                                         │
    └─────────────────────────────────────────────────────────┘
    ```

3. How do these words add interest and meaning to the writing?

    _____

    _____

4. What details would you like to see the author add to the narrative?

    _____

    _____

➤ Part Two

Read the statements that describe the qualities of narrative writing.

1. Color the box next to each statement to show how well the author wrote that part of his or her narrative paragraph.

    *   Color the box *blue* for excellent writing of that part of the paragraph.
    *   Color the box *green* for writing that meets that quality of narrative writing.
    *   Color the box *yellow* for writing that could be strengthened in that area.

The topic sentence introduces the character(s), the setting, and the experience the narrative will describe.	
The actions that are part of the experience are in an order that makes sense.	
Description and action are used to describe an experience.	
Concrete words and details describe what happens during the experience.	
Transition words are used to guide readers through the actions.	
The concluding sentence flows naturally from the experience.	

2. Write a clear, kind suggestion for any qualities you colored yellow. Look at the words that describe the quality for ideas about how your classmate could strengthen his or her writing.

    _____

    _____

Second Draft and Self-Evaluation

➤ Objective

Students will discuss their first drafts with partners and make revision notes. They will write second drafts of their narratives and use a rubric to evaluate each part of their paragraphs for effective narrative writing.

➤ Introduction

You will use the notes from your first draft to write a second draft. Then you will use a rubric to look closely at strengths and weaknesses in your writing.

➤ Instruction

The second draft gives writers the chance to continue to make their writing stronger. One way to make our writing stronger is to check grammar and how sentences are put together. Make sure sentences start in different ways. This keeps your writing interesting for readers. Reread your topic sentence. Can readers tell what experience your narrative will describe? Does your sentence tell readers where the experience takes place? Check for words that invite readers to use their senses to imagine what happens. Did you use concrete words to show readers what you are writing about?

➤ Guided Practice

We use conventions to make our writing correct. Some conventions are capitalization, punctuation, and spelling. When these things are correct, writing is easier to read and understand. Talk with a partner about things you can change in your first drafts. Help each other find things that need to be corrected. Look at the way sentences are put together and the words you used. Check capital letters, punctuation, and spelling. Look also at the comments you received on "Peer Review" (page 124). Mark things you would like to change in your first draft. Then write a second draft of your narrative paragraph.

➤ Independent Practice

Distribute "Self-Evaluation: Narrative Paragraph" (page 126). *Read the first row of the rubric. Look at the topic sentence of your second draft. Which box in this row best describes your sentence? Write notes about what you would like to change to make your writing more closely match the quality of a high-scoring topic sentence. Read one row of the rubric at a time. Check your paragraph for each quality of strong narrative writing. Write notes about changes you would like to make to your second draft. Then score your second draft.*

➤ Review

Discuss the impact revising has on the writing process. Review specific categories of the rubric, as needed, to guide students as they write their second drafts. Provide examples of specific sentences for each part of a narrative paragraph that would receive a high score according to the description(s) on the rubric.

➤ Closing

You looked at your notes and comments from a partner. You wrote a second draft of your narrative. Then you used a rubric to think about changes you want to make to your writing to make it stronger.

Self-Evaluation: Narrative Paragraph

Name: _____ **Score:** _____

	4	3	2	1
Topic Sentence	My narrative has a topic sentence that introduces a narrator and/or characters, a setting, and an experience observing an animal in nature.	My narrative has a topic sentence that introduces a narrator, a setting, and an experience observing an animal.	My narrative has a topic sentence that introduces a character who narrates an experience.	My narrative does not have a topic sentence nor does it introduce the narrator, characters, setting, or experience.
Organization	My narrator describes an experience observing an animal in nature in an order that makes sense.	My narrator describes an experience observing an animal.	My narrator describes an experience, but it is not told in an order that makes sense.	My narrative does not describe an experience.
Action	I use description and action to describe an experience observing an animal in nature and to show how characters respond.	I use description and action to describe an experience observing an animal.	I use action or description to describe an experience.	I do not use action or description well to describe an experience.
Concrete Words and Details	I include concrete words and sensory details to describe an experience observing an animal in nature.	I include concrete words or sensory details to describe an experience observing an animal.	I include details to describe an experience.	I do not include specific details to describe an experience.
Transition Words	I use transition words and phrases to guide readers through a logical sequence of actions within the experience.	I use transition words in some places to show the order of actions within the experience.	I use transition words once or twice to show the order of actions within the experience.	I do not use transition words to show the order of actions within the experience.
Concluding Sentence	My narrative has a concluding sentence that flows naturally from the narrated experience and provides a sense of closure.	My narrative has a concluding sentence that describes the end of the experience.	My narrative has a concluding sentence.	My narrative does not have a concluding sentence.

Final Draft

➤ Objective

Students will refer to their notes and self-evaluations to write final drafts using digital tools. Then they will review their final drafts and answer questions about the purpose of an audience for their narrative paragraphs.

➤ Introduction

You will use the notes you wrote on your second draft to write a final draft. You will use digital tools to write this final copy. Then you will read your final draft to yourself and answer questions about your narrative.

➤ Instruction

The final draft of a narrative piece is the copy we will share with an audience. We want our writing to be easy for readers to understand. Think about the experience your narrative describes. Who would most enjoy reading it? A final draft is stronger than a first draft. The final copy shows writing that has been read and edited more than one time.

➤ Guided Practice

Often we share our final copy with an audience. This is called publishing our writing. Who is our audience? Think about the people who will be interested in reading your paragraph. We can also think about the places people read writing. Brainstorm with students places they can publish their narrative paragraphs, such as a school newspaper, classroom or school library book, or as a book to read to younger students during a study of animals. Distribute students' copies of "Self-Evaluation: Narrative Paragraph" (page 126). *Look at the notes you made on your second draft about changes you want to make. Then write your final draft.* Provide resources for students to use digital tools to compose their final drafts, such as a word-processing program, note program, interactive whiteboard file or flipchart page, access to a class blog, or a shared document.

➤ Independent Practice

Distribute "Examine Your Writing" (page 128). *Think about why you wrote about this experience. Who would like to read your narrative? Answer the questions. Whisper-read your final draft with your audience in mind.*

➤ Review

Review possible audiences and reasons for writing a narrative paragraph about an experience observing an animal in nature. Discuss with the class before or after students compose their final drafts. Provide digital tools and resources for student publishing, as available.

➤ Closing

You looked at the notes you wrote on your second draft to write a final draft of your narrative paragraph. You answered questions to think about your audience and why you wrote about this experience. Then you whisper-read your final copy with your audience in mind.

Name(s): _____

Examine Your Writing

Review and reflect on your final draft. Answer the questions on the lines below each magnifying glass. Then whisper-read your final draft with your audience in mind.

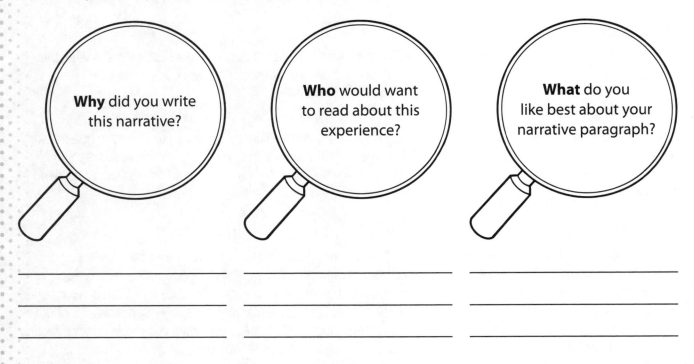

Why did you write this narrative?

_____

_____

_____

_____

Who would want to read about this experience?

_____

_____

_____

_____

What do you like best about your narrative paragraph?

_____

_____

_____

_____

What would you like to do better next time?

_____

_____

_____

What will readers remember after they read your animal experience narrative?

_____

_____

_____

Final Evaluation

➤ Objective

Students will create line graphs to show feedback they received from classmates, the scores from their self-evaluations, and the scores they received from the teacher. They will then answer reflection questions about the strengths and weaknesses in their writing as identified on the graphs.

➤ Introduction

Today you will use a graph to compare the scores you gave your paragraph with the scores I gave your writing. You will also look at the comments you received from classmates. Then you will answer questions about what you noticed on the chart.

➤ Instruction

People use graphs to see information at a glance. Display the line graph from "A Picture of My Scores" (page 131). *What do you notice about the graph? The words at the bottom of the graph describe parts of a narrative paragraph. The numbers on the left side match the scores on the rubric. We will use this graph to compare information from different sources. You will compare the comments you received from classmates with rubric scores you received. This graph will help you compare your scores for the qualities of strong narrative writing.*

➤ Guided Practice

Make sure students have their copies of "Peer Review" (page 124), "Self-Evaluation: Narrative Paragraph" (page 126), and "Teacher Evaluation: Narrative Paragraph" (page 130). Distribute "A Picture of My Scores." Distribute colored pencils. *Look at the boxes a classmate colored on "Peer Review." These boxes are like scores from your partner. Which parts of your narrative have blue boxes?* Model how to find the intersection of the category and the line for a score of "4" for students. *Draw a dot on the line that shows a score of "4" above those parts. Draw a dot on the "3" line for any qualities that have green boxes. For any qualities that have a yellow box, draw a dot on the "2" or "1" line. Draw lines to connect the dots to see a picture of areas of strengths and weaknesses in your paragraph. Next, look at the scores you gave your narrative paragraph on the self-evaluation. Find your score for each quality on the rubric. Use a different color for these dots. Draw a dot on the line that matches the score you gave your writing for that part of your paragraph. Draw lines to connect these dots. Now look at the scores I gave your writing on the teacher evaluation. Use a different color for the dots. For each quality on the rubric, draw a dot on the line that matches the score you received for that part of your paragraph. Draw lines to connect the dots. This will show you a picture of strengths and weaknesses your teacher noticed in your writing.*

➤ Independent Practice

Look at the high points and low points in the lines you drew on the graph on page 131. This shows how your scores compare. Then answer the questions in Part Two.

➤ Review

Review specific categories of the rubric to help students understand their scores on the teacher evaluation. Model how to plot a simple line graph and draw connecting lines to see patterns. Think aloud to make comparisons between data represented on such a graph.

➤ Closing

You looked at the scores you received from different people. You used a line graph to compare the scores. You also answered questions to think about what you learned about the strengths and weaknesses in your writing.

Teacher Evaluation: Narrative Paragraph

Student Name: _____ **Score:** _____

	4	3	2	1
Topic Sentence	The narrative has a topic sentence that introduces a narrator and/or characters, a setting, and an experience observing an animal in nature.	The narrative has a topic sentence that introduces a narrator, a setting, and an experience observing an animal.	The narrative has a topic sentence that introduces a character who narrates an experience.	The narrative does not have a topic sentence nor does it introduce the narrator, characters, setting, or experience.
Organization	The narrator describes an experience observing an animal in nature in an order that makes sense.	The narrator describes an experience observing an animal.	The narrator describes an experience, but it is not told in an order that makes sense.	The narrative does not describe an experience.
Action	The author uses description and action to describe an experience observing an animal in nature and to show how characters respond.	The author uses description and action to describe an experience observing an animal.	The author uses action or description to describe an experience.	The author does not use action or description well to describe an experience.
Concrete Words and Details	The author includes concrete words and sensory details to describe an experience observing an animal in nature.	The author includes concrete words or sensory details to describe an experience observing an animal.	The author includes details to describe an experience.	The author does not include specific details to describe an experience.
Transition Words	The author uses transition words and phrases to guide readers through a logical sequence of actions within the experience.	The author uses transition words in some places to show the order of actions within the experience.	The author uses transition words once or twice to show the order of actions within the experience.	The author does not use transition words to show the order of actions within the experience.
Concluding Sentence	The narrative has a concluding sentence that flows naturally from the narrated experience and provides a sense of closure.	The narrative has a concluding sentence that describes the end of the experience.	The narrative has a concluding sentence.	The narrative does not have a concluding sentence.

Name(s): _____

A Picture of My Scores

➤ Part One

1. Look at the boxes a classmate colored on "Peer Review" (page 124). These boxes are like scores from your partner.

   Which parts of your narrative have blue boxes? Draw a dot on the line that shows a score of "4" above those parts. Draw a dot on the "3" line for any qualities that have green boxes. For qualities that have a yellow box, draw a dot on the "2" or "1" line. Draw lines to connect the dots to see a picture of areas of strengths and weaknesses in your paragraph.

2. Look at the scores you gave your narrative paragraph on "Self-Evaluation: Narrative Paragraph" (page 126).

   Find your score for each quality on the rubric. Use a different color for these dots. Draw a dot on the line that matches the score you gave your writing for that part of your paragraph. Draw lines to connect these dots.

3. Look at the scores you received on your narrative paragraph on "Teacher Evaluation: Narrative Paragraph" (page 130).

   Use a different color for these dots. For each quality on the rubric, draw a dot on the line that matches the score you received for that part of your paragraph. Draw lines to connect the dots. This will show you a picture of strengths and weaknesses your teacher noticed in your writing.

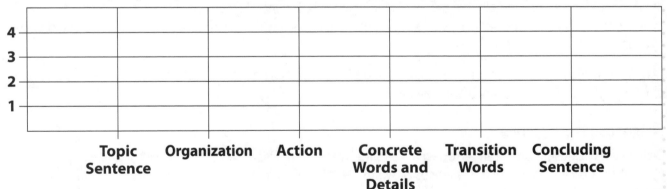

➤ Part Two

Look at the high points and low points in the lines you drew on the graph. This shows how your scores compare. Answer the following questions on a separate piece of paper.

1. What do you notice from the graph of your scores?

2. Which area(s) have the closest scores?

3. Which area(s) have scores that are farther apart?

4. Why do you think the difference(s) happened?

5. Look at the graph. What areas will you work to strengthen when you write a narrative essay in the next module?

Review

➤ Objective

Students will use hand motions to demonstrate their understanding of the parts of a narrative paragraph as an example is read aloud. Then they will read the sample paragraph and identify the topic sentence, details, and concluding sentence, and discuss in small groups changes they could make to strengthen the writing.

➤ Introduction

Before today, you wrote a narrative paragraph about observing an animal in nature. Today you will read an example of a narrative paragraph. You will think about the qualities of narrative writing in the paragraph. Then you will talk with classmates in a small group about how you could improve the writing.

➤ Instruction

Narrative writing describes a real or imagined experience. The things that happen are told in order. Authors use concrete words and details to describe the actions. The topic sentence lets readers know who is telling the story and where the story takes place. Details and words that use the senses help readers imagine they are part of the experience. Sentences have transition words to show the order in which actions happen. A strong concluding sentence ends the experience. It makes sense because of the actions that happened.

➤ Guided Practice

Let's think of hand movements we could use to show each feature of narrative writing (for example, a single hand wave to introduce a character; the waving of both hands to show the setting; hands to eyes or ears to show sensory details; one hand across the other in a chopping motion to show concrete word choice; fingers walking to show events or actions in a narrative; hands crossed across chest to show transition words; hands spread out to show a natural concluding sentence).

Display "An Unusual Chick" (page 133). *Listen carefully as I read this narrative paragraph. Show the correct hand motion as you hear each quality of narrative writing.*

➤ Independent Practice

Distribute "An Unusual Chick" and "Review a Narrative" (page 134). *Read the paragraph with your small group. Then you will work on your own. Write sentences or words near the picture in Part One to tell the parts of this narrative paragraph. First find the topic sentence. Write it near the part of the picture that says "topic sentence." Then look for details about the five senses and concrete words that describe things. Write them in the place that says "descriptive words." Find the actions and the concluding sentence. Copy them in the correct places on the activity page. Compare your answers with your small group. What changes would you make to the narrative to make it more interesting? Talk about your ideas with your small group. In Part Two, write notes about the changes you and your classmates would make to the narrative to make it more interesting for readers.*

➤ Review

Read narrative samples from classroom materials or anonymous student writing to give students additional practice identifying qualities of narrative writing.

➤ Closing

You read an example of a narrative paragraph. Then you pointed out each quality of narrative writing in the paragraph. You talked about the narrative with classmates and brainstormed ways to improve the writing.

Name(s): _____

An Unusual Chick

The most unusual animal I have ever seen outside of a zoo is an albatross chick. My family was on a beautiful island near the ocean. We were on our way to the trail that led to the beach. As we walked through the neighborhood, we saw a strange bird sitting on a lawn. It had a fuzzy head and long beak. It looked like a chick, but it was a very big chick. We stopped to take its picture. It sat very still, and we tried not to frighten it. Later, we looked at a book. We discovered it was a baby albatross. I don't know why it didn't fly away when we got near. But I'm glad I got to see it up close!

Teacher Notes
Grade level: appropriate
Lexile estimate: 540L

Name(s): _____

Review a Narrative

➤ Part One

1. Read "An Unusual Chick" (page 133).

2. Write the sentence or words near the parts of the picture below to tell the main parts of this narrative paragraph.

Topic Sentence

_____

_____

_____

_____

Actions

_____

_____

_____

_____

Descriptive Words

_____

_____

_____

_____

_____

Concluding Sentence

_____

_____

_____

_____

➤ Part Two

1. Compare your answers with classmates in a small group.

2. What changes would you make to the narrative to make it more interesting for readers? Talk about your ideas with your small group.

3. In the box below, write notes about the changes you and your classmates would make to the narrative to make it more interesting for readers.

```
┌──────────────────────────────────────────────┐
│                                                │
│                                                │
│                                                │
│                                                │
│                                                │
└──────────────────────────────────────────────┘
```

Introductory Paragraphs

➤ Objective

Students will share titles and clues with classmates to generate ideas to write introductory paragraphs for their narrative essays. They will also view images (photographs from home or illustrations from similar stories in books or other media sources) related to family stories, describe the narrative events to partners, and sequence event ideas for their narratives.

➤ Introduction

In this module, you will plan and write a narrative about something interesting that happened in your or another person's family. Your narrative will begin with an introductory paragraph.

➤ Instruction

An introductory paragraph is the first paragraph of a longer narrative. Authors let readers know who is telling the story and where it takes place. The person telling the story is called the narrator. There may also be other people, or characters, who are part of the experience. This paragraph also tells readers the main event or problem that happens. It is important for this paragraph to be interesting and catch readers' attention so they will want to keep reading.

➤ Guided Practice

Distribute "Clues to My Narrative" (page 136). *Think about an interesting thing that happened in your or another person's family. Then write a title for your narrative. Write clues to help classmates guess what your narrative will be about. Who is telling the story? Where did it happen? The place is the setting for your story. What are the main events that happened? Writing the clues will help you think about your story. Share your title and clues. Ask classmates to guess what your narrative will be about. Then write sentences about the character(s), setting, and events in your story. Trade papers with a classmate. Read your classmate's sentences. Then write questions you have about your classmate's story after reading his or her sentences. Give your partner's paper back. Read your partner's questions or comments. Rewrite your sentences to make them more interesting for readers.*

➤ Independent Practice

Distribute "Picture My Narrative" (page 137). *Look at a photograph that reminds you of the family story you will describe in your narrative. If you do not have a family picture, look at a picture from a book or other source (Internet or video clip). Find a picture that shows where the story took place. Work with a partner. Take turns telling each other about the characters, setting, and story event(s) in each of your narratives. Trade papers with your partner. Listen carefully as your partner describes his or her idea for a family story. In Part One, write the main ideas and important words you hear. If you do not know all of the words, draw a picture. This will help your partner remember his or her thoughts. Give your partner's paper back to him or her. Read the comments from your partner. Brainstorm ideas about what happens in your narrative. Write one event in each box in Part Two. Number the boxes to show the order in which events happen in the story.*

➤ Review

Use the whole-group activity to prompt a class discussion about how authors introduce a narrative, for example, by asking questions about characters, the setting, and story events.

➤ Closing

You wrote a sample title and clues about your narrative. Then you asked classmates to guess what your story is about. You also wrote sentences for the introductory paragraph of your essay. You looked at pictures for ideas and brainstormed events that will happen in your narrative.

Clues to My Narrative

Write a title for your narrative story about an interesting family experience on the line below.

_____

Write other clues to help classmates guess what your narrative will be about.

1. _____

2. _____

3. _____

Share your title and clues and ask classmates to guess what your narrative will be about.

Use the title, clues you wrote, and feedback from classmates to write sentences to introduce your story.

_____

_____

_____

_____

_____

Trade papers with a classmate to read each other's introductory sentences.

In the box below, write questions you have about your classmate's story after reading his or her sentences. If your reader is asking questions, that's good. It means they want to find out more about what happens in your story.

```
┌─────────────────────────────────────────────────────────┐
│                                                           │
│                                                           │
│                                                           │
│                                                           │
└─────────────────────────────────────────────────────────┘
```

Now rewrite your sentences to make them more interesting for readers.

_____

_____

_____

_____

Name(s): _____

Picture My Narrative

➤ Part One

1. Look at a photograph that reminds you of the family story you will describe in your narrative.

    If you do not have a family picture, look at a picture from a book or other source (Internet or video clip). Find a picture that shows where a story took place.

2. Tell your partner about the characters, setting, and story event in your narrative.

3. Trade papers. Listen carefully as your partner describes his or her idea for a narrative about a family story. In the box below, write the main ideas and important words you hear.

    If you do not know all of the words, draw a picture to help your partner remember his or her thoughts.

➤ Part Two

Read the comments from your partner. Brainstorm ideas about what happens in your narrative. Write one event in each box. Number the boxes in the top left corner to show the order in which events happen in the story.

Body Paragraphs

➤ Objective

Students will participate in a role-play activity to think about dialogue in their narratives and then share descriptive words in small groups. They will also think about the actions that are part of the events that take place in their narrative experiences.

➤ Introduction

You will act out the things characters will say and do in your narrative. Then you will share words that describe the actions. You will also write sentences about the actions that are part of the things that happen in your narrative.

➤ Instruction

People do different things when something happens to them. In a narrative, characters talk or act when an event happens. When characters talk, we call this dialogue. Authors use dialogue and descriptive words to show what characters say and do in a narrative. We can use words that show how characters use their senses. This helps readers picture the details of the setting and experience. Strong narrative writing shows readers what the characters see, hear, smell, taste, touch, feel, and experience. In the last module, you wrote a narrative paragraph. We learned that transition words show how much time has gone by. Transition words can also show characters moving from one place to another. These words show events in an experience in an order that makes sense. This helps readers follow the action.

➤ Guided Practice

Distribute "What People Say" (page 139). *In Part One, draw two characters (as stick people) in your narrative. What do they say to each other in the story experience? Write your ideas in the speech bubbles. Share your ideas with two or three classmates. Act out what happens. What do you need to change or add to the dialogue? Write notes in the speech bubbles in Part Two.*

➤ Independent Practice

Distribute "Describing the Experience" (page 140). *Write a sentence to tell readers about your character(s), setting, and experience. Look at the ideas you wrote on "Clues to My Narrative" (page 136), if necessary. Read your sentence(s) to a small group. Ask each person in the group to share one or more words to describe the experience you are writing about. Write the words in the circles. After everyone in the group has shared their sentences, work on your own. Add detail words to the ideas you received from your classmates. Rewrite your sentences on the lines.*

Display "Action Steps" (page 141). *What happens in the experience your narrative will describe? Let's think about the experience of getting a new pet. What is the most important event or moment? We'll write the event of bringing home our new pet in the top box. What has to happen first before we can bring home a new pet? We can write that we have to buy food for our pet in the box below that leads up to it. Let's think about the dialogue and what your characters would be doing.* Record student responses for sample dialogue and actions. *Continue to write actions that have to happen in order for something else to happen in the story. Work backwards through the story to get to the first action or event that will happen in the narrative. Then go back and write one or more descriptive action words in each box.* Distribute "Action Steps" and assist students as they complete the graphic organizer for their narrative essays.

➤ Review

Provide appropriate dictionaries and other resources for students to review action words for the events in their narratives. Talk through the process of working backwards through the events leading up to the most important event to scaffold and model for students.

➤ Closing

You wrote notes about what the characters in your narrative will say. Then you shared action words with classmates to describe what happens in a narrative. You also thought about the order of events in your narrative.

Name(s): _____

What People Say

➤ Part One

1. Draw and label stick figures for two characters in your narrative.

2. What do they say to each other in the story experience you will describe? Write your ideas in the speech bubbles below.

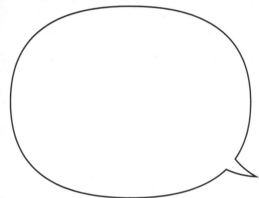 

➤ Part Two

1. Share your ideas with two or three classmates.

2. Act out what happens. What do you need to change or add to the dialogue? Write notes about what you will change or add in the speech bubbles below.

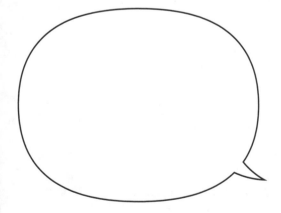 

Name(s): _____

Describing the Experience

Write a sentence that introduces your character(s), setting, and narrative experience. Refer to the ideas you wrote on "Clues to My Narrative" (page 136), if necessary.

_____

_____

_____

Read your sentence(s) to a small group. Ask each person in the group to share one or more descriptive words that relate to your narrative. Write the words in the circles.

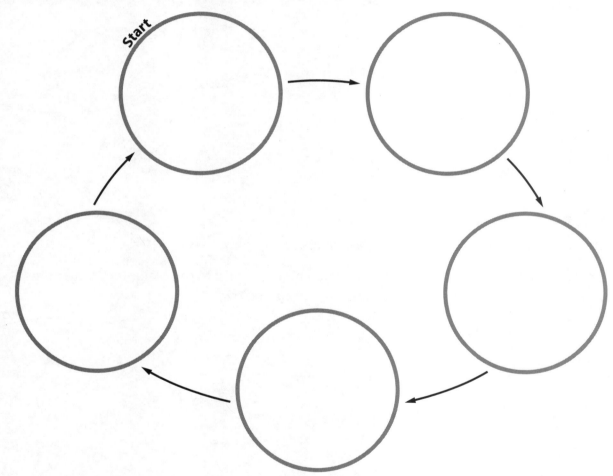

After everyone in the group has shared sentences related to their narratives, work on your own to add descriptive words to the ideas you received from your classmates. Rewrite your sentence(s) here.

_____

_____

_____

Action Steps

1. What happens in the experience your narrative will describe? What is the most important event or moment? Write the most important event or moment in the top box.

2. What has to happen first before that event can happen? Write an action in the box below that leads up to it.

3. Continue to write actions that have to happen next in order for something else to happen in the story.

4. Work backwards through the story to get to the first action or event that will happen in the narrative.

5. Start with the first "step" and write one or more action words in the box. Think about any words that describe the action and write those words as well. Then add action words to the other event boxes.

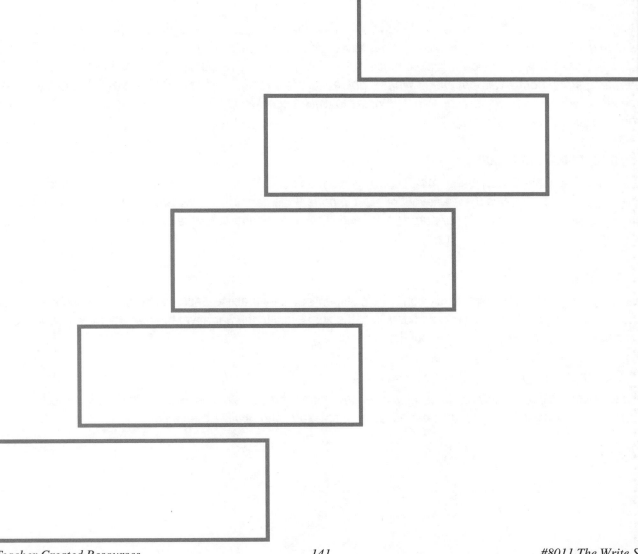

Conclusions

➤ Objective

Students will read a sample narrative essay, discuss ideas for a conclusion, and write conclusions. Then they will brainstorm ideas for the final events in their own narratives on a graphic organizer and use their notes to draft conclusions.

➤ Introduction

You will read an example of a narrative. You will talk with classmates about ideas for the ending. Then you will write a conclusion for the narrative. You will also brainstorm ideas for a conclusion for your own narrative. You will write a conclusion for your narrative.

➤ Instruction

Strong narrative writing makes readers care about the characters and what happens to them. What happens to the characters may change the way readers think. The conclusion in a narrative is the end of the experience. The narrator may say how this experience changed the way he or she thinks. The ending of a narrative may describe a lesson the narrator learned. The narrator may describe how he or she will do things differently now.

➤ Guided Practice

Distribute "A Great Family Experience" (page 143). *Read the sample narrative with your small group. Talk about what might happen as the final event in the narrative. Write one idea you think would be a good ending. Then talk with classmates about how this experience might change the way readers think or act. What do you think the narrator learned from what happened? What might readers learn from reading the narrative? Write notes in the spaces on your activity page. Then use your notes to write a conclusion for the narrative. If you have time, share your conclusion with your group.*

➤ Independent Practice

Distribute "The Final Event" (page 144). *Look at your notes from "Picture My Narrative" (page 137) and "Action Steps" (page 141). What is the final event or most important moment of your narrative experience? Complete the graphic organizer to plan how your narrative will end. Then use a separate piece of paper to write a conclusion for your narrative.*

➤ Review

Review the characteristics of a conclusion to help students as they practice writing conclusions during the activities. (The narrator describes the actions and details of the final event in the narrative; the narrator may include a sentence about how he or she felt about the experience.)

➤ Closing

You practiced writing a conclusion for a sample narrative. Then you brainstormed ideas for the ending of your narrative. You wrote a conclusion for your own narrative about an interesting family experience.

Name(s): _____

A Great Family Experience

Over spring break my family went to an amusement park. The drive was boring, but the rides were awesome! I got to go on a lot of exciting rides. My favorite ride was the roller coaster.

The roller coaster is a great ride. But one bad thing is that it is very popular, so it has a very long line. This roller coaster went upside down. I thought it went very fast.

After that, I went on another roller coaster ride. It was called the Grizzly. First the cars go slowly up a hill. Then the Grizzly turns to the right and goes down. It comes to a quick halt at the end. I rode this ride at least four times.

When it was time for lunch, we took a break and had a picnic. We found a table that was partly in the sun and partly in the shade. My grandparents sat on the shady side. Mom, my brother, and I sat on the sunny side. We enjoyed our ham sandwiches and fruit.

After you have read the essay above, answer the following questions:

- What did the narrator learn from the experience?

  _____

  _____

- What might readers learn from the narrative?

  _____

  _____

Then, on another piece of paper, write a conclusion for the narrative.

Teacher Notes

Grade level: appropriate
Lexile estimate: 490L

Name(s): _____

The Final Event

1. Look at your notes from "Picture My Narrative" (page 137) and "Action Steps" (page 141).

2. Complete the graphic organizer to plan how your narrative will end.

3. Use these notes to write a conclusion for your narrative on a separate piece of paper.

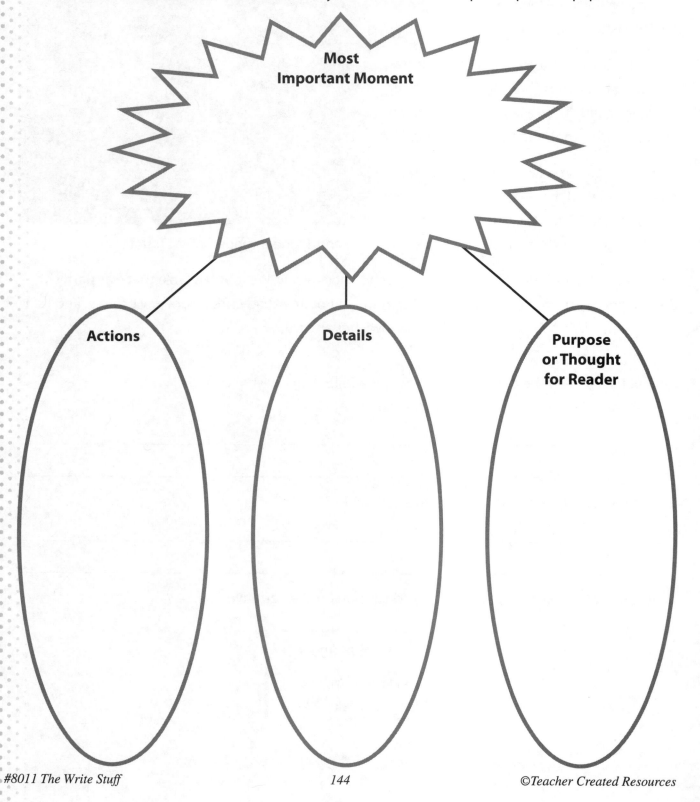

First Draft and Peer Review

➤ Objective

Students will write first drafts of their narrative essays and then participate in a peer-review activity to give and receive feedback on their writing.

➤ Introduction

You will use your notes and writing from activities you have already done in this module. You will write a first draft of your narrative about an interesting family experience. Then you will read your writing to a partner. You will give and receive comments to help you make your narrative stronger.

➤ Instruction

A first draft puts together all the notes and ideas into one complete narrative. You will look at your notes and practice sentences from activities you have already done. Then you will write the first draft of your narrative. Your introductory paragraph is the first paragraph. It will tell readers about the narrator, setting, and experience. The body paragraphs will tell what happened during the experience. You will describe the events in the order they happened. Use concrete words to describe the experience. Include dialogue and actions to show what characters did and said when things happened. Your conclusion will be your last paragraph. Write a conclusion that ends the narrative in a way that makes sense. The conclusion may also give readers something to think about.

➤ Guided Practice

Guide students through writing the first drafts of their narrative essays. Distribute students' copies of "Clues to My Narrative" (page 136), "Picture My Narrative" (page 137), "What People Say" (page 139), "Describing the Experience" (page 140), "Action Steps" (page 141), and "The Final Event" (page 144). *Think of an interesting way to start your narrative. Make sure your introductory paragraph tells readers about the narrator, setting, and the experience you will describe. Write sentences about the events that happen in an order that makes sense. Remember to use dialogue and actions to show what the characters say and do. Use your notes from "The Final Event" to write a conclusion for your narrative.*

➤ Independent Practice

Distribute "Helping Each Other Write" (page 146). *Trade papers with a classmate. Listen as your partner reads his or her first draft out loud. Retell what you heard your partner say. Describe any pictures you saw in your mind when you heard the narrative. Tell your partner which parts you would like to know more about. Color the stars next to each quality of narrative writing to show how closely your partner's narrative matches that quality. This will show your partner areas in which he or she might want to improve his or her writing.*

➤ Review

Review how students can use the feedback they receive from a classmate to revise and improve their narratives.

➤ Closing

You wrote the first draft of your narrative. You received comments about strengths and weaknesses in your writing.

Helping Each Other Write

Trade papers with a classmate Listen as your partner reads his or her first draft out loud. Then complete the activity.

1. Retell your partner's experience in your own words. What did you hear your partner say?

    _____

    _____

2. Describe the pictures you had in your mind as your partner read.

see	
hear	
smell	
touch	
taste	

3. Tell your partner which parts you would like to know more about.

    _____

    _____

4. Color the stars (three for "strong" and one for "needs work") next to each quality of narrative writing to show how closely your partner's narrative matches that quality.

☆ ☆ ☆	The introductory paragraph tells about the narrator, setting, and experience.
☆ ☆ ☆	Body paragraphs describe what happens in the narrative experience.
☆ ☆ ☆	Events are described in an order that makes sense.
☆ ☆ ☆	Concrete words and sensory details describe the experience.
☆ ☆ ☆	Dialogue and actions show what characters said and did.
☆ ☆ ☆	The conclusion ends the narrative in a way that makes sense.
☆ ☆ ☆	The conclusion leaves readers with something to think about.

Second Draft and Self-Evaluation

➤ Objective

Students will use feedback from peers, notes, and suggestions to revise their narratives and write second drafts. Then they will use a rubric to evaluate their second drafts and write comments about their writing in preparation to write final drafts.

➤ Introduction

You will think about the comments you have heard from classmates about your writing. You will also look at notes you have made about things you would like to change. Then you will write a second draft of your narrative. You will use a rubric to look closely at your writing. You will write comments about things you want to change when you write your final draft.

➤ Instruction

Authors write more than one draft of a narrative. This helps them make their writing easy for readers to understand. Think about the qualities of effective narrative writing as you write your second draft. Use concrete words to describe people, places, and things. This gives readers pictures in their minds of the experiences. Detail words show what a character sees, hears, smells, tastes, or touches. Use action and dialogue to show what characters do and say when things happen. Make sure the events in your experience are in an order that makes sense. Are there any places that need more details to make it more interesting or easy to understand?

➤ Guided Practice

Distribute students' copies of "Helping Each Other Write" (page 146). *Look at the comments you received from a partner. Think about what you might add to your ideas. How can you organize your narrative to make it interesting and easier for readers to understand? Read your introductory paragraph. Which sentence would most grab readers' attention? You might want to put your sentences in a different order to hook the reader. Now read your body paragraphs. How well do your details describe the experience? Did you show what characters do and say when things happen to them? Look over your conclusion. What effect will your narrative have on readers? What will they remember after they read your writing? Then write a second draft of your narrative. Use the comments you have received, your notes, and these suggestions to help you.*

➤ Independent Practice

Distribute "Self-Evaluation: Narrative Essay" (page 148) and small sticky notes to each student. Read one row of the rubric and discuss the scores that show different levels of quality for that characteristic. *Read one row of the rubric at a time. Look at that part of your narrative. Decide which description best matches your writing for that quality of narrative writing. Place a sticky note in the square that best describes your narrative. On the sticky note, write a comment about your writing. What did you do well in this part of your narrative? What would you like to do better? If you don't have room on the sticky note to write your comment, write a number. Then write a comment for each number on a separate piece of paper. Score your second draft.*

➤ Review

Discuss the impact revising has on the writing process. Review specific categories of the rubric, as needed, to guide students as they write their second drafts. Demonstrate how to write comments on sticky notes or numbers and numbered comments. Review the meaning of writing conventions with students. Go over this part of the rubric and model checking for correct conventions, as needed.

➤ Closing

Use your self-evaluation and notes to write a final draft of your narrative essay. Bring it back to class for the following lesson.

Self-Evaluation: Narrative Essay

Name: _____   Score: _____

	4	3	2	1
Narrator and/or Characters	My narrative introduces a narrator and/or characters who had an interesting family experience.	My narrative introduces a narrator and/or characters who had a family experience.	My narrative introduces a character who narrates an experience.	My narrative does not introduce the narrator or any characters.
Setting and Situation	My narrative introduces a setting and situation about an interesting family experience to orient my readers.	My narrative introduces a situation about a family experience.	My narrative introduces a setting, but the situation is unclear.	My narrative does not introduce a setting or a situation.
Organization	My narrator describes events in an interesting family experience in an order that makes sense.	My narrator describes events in a family experience.	My narrator describes events in a family experience, but they are not in an order that makes sense.	My narrative does not describe events.
Dialogue and/or Description	I use dialogue and description to describe an interesting family experience and to show how characters respond.	I use dialogue and description to describe a family experience.	I use dialogue or description to describe an experience.	I do not use dialogue or description well to describe an experience.
Details	I include concrete words and sensory details to describe events in my narrative about an interesting family experience.	I include concrete words or sensory details to describe events in my narrative about a family experience.	I include details to describe events in my narrative about an experience.	I do not include specific details to describe events in my narrative.
Transition Words	I use transition words to guide readers through the sequence of events.	I use transition words in some places to show the order of events.	I use transition words once or twice to show the order of events.	I do not use transition words to show the order of events.
Conclusion	My narrative has a conclusion that flows naturally from the narrated experience and provides a sense of closure.	My narrative has a conclusion that describes the end of the experience.	My narrative has a conclusion.	My narrative does not have a satisfactory conclusion.
Conventions	My narrative has correct writing conventions.	My narrative has a few writing errors, but they do not affect the meaning.	My narrative has writing errors that need editing because they make my writing hard to understand.	My narrative has many writing errors that change the meaning of what I want to say.

Review

➤ Objective

Students will participate in a class discussion to review qualities of narrative writing. Then they will read a sample narrative and identify specific words and sentences that exemplify the qualities of narrative writing and make suggestions to strengthen the writing.

➤ Introduction

You will talk about the qualities of narrative writing with classmates. Then you will read a sample narrative and write key words to show those qualities in the sample. You will also think about what you have learned about narrative writing. Then you will brainstorm ways the sample narrative could be stronger.

➤ Instruction

One way to learn about certain types of writing is to study models. You have learned about narrative writing. You know some things to notice in this type of writing. We can look at the qualities on the rubrics to remember what we have learned. This will help us notice how well an author included these qualities in his or her writing.

➤ Guided Practice

Display "The Keys to a Great Experience" (page 151). *What are the qualities of strong narrative writing? What happens in the first paragraph of a narrative?* (The author introduces the narrator, setting, and situation.) *What will we find in the body paragraphs?* (They contain events described in order; details about characters, setting, and things that happened; and dialogue and actions that show what characters do and say as a result of the events in the experience.) *Why do authors include details about the senses?* (This shows readers what characters see, hear, smell, taste, and touch; it helps readers become part of the experience.) *What have we learned about the concluding paragraph?* (It describes the final event in the experience and provides an end to the narrative; it shows why the experience is interesting or important for readers.) Work together with students to write qualities of narrative writing on the keys. Keep the examples posted for student reference during Independent Practice.

➤ Independent Practice

Distribute "Birthday Contest" (page 150) and "The Keys to a Great Experience." *Read the sample narrative. Look at the qualities of narrative writing we listed together in class. Then write words and sentences from the narrative to show each part of narrative writing. How would you change this narrative to make it stronger? Write your ideas on the activity page.*

➤ Review

Go over the sample narrative with students and discuss ways the writing could be strengthened (a clearer introduction of setting, more details, more specific actions, more details and description in the conclusion about the final event in the narrative, perhaps improve reader interest).

➤ Closing

You have talked about the qualities of narrative writing with classmates. Then you read a sample narrative. You wrote examples of the qualities of narrative writing from the sample.

Name(s): _____

Birthday Contest

I could hardly wait for my cousins to arrive for the birthday contest. Every year, we have a contest to see who could make the best creation using food items. Our contest had rules and prizes. We worked in teams.

"They're here!" My sister ran to open the door. I followed, curious to see what Hannah and Sarah had brought to help us create. Maybe this year would be different and my aunt would put some fruity candy in for a change. I watched as Hannah and my sister spilled the bags onto the kitchen counter.

Small bags of raisins and nuts spilled out. "What will we start with?" We weren't making gingerbread houses, but we needed something to build with.

"Celery! Carrots!" Sarah held up pre-cut sticks and hopped around. Carrots were my favorite healthy food, but I didn't know what we could make.

Hannah reached for a bowl of blueberries. As she started to pull it toward her, it tipped over and blueberries rolled all over the counter. "Quick! Stop them before they fall on the floor!" Sarah stretched out her arms to catch the berries.

Mom divided us into teams, each of us with one of the cousins. I always worked with Sarah. We put our heads together and looked over the choices. "What do you think about building a bridge?" I asked.

Sarah moved some things around as she thought. Then she started putting different foods together. I watched until I figured it out. "Smart! I like your idea!" I smiled at her and began to help her build our scene.

Teacher Notes

Grade level: appropriate

Lexile estimate: 560L

Name(s): _____

The Keys to a Great Experience

1. Read "Birthday Contest" (page 150).
2. Look at the qualities of narrative writing listed during the class discussion.
3. Find examples of each part of narrative writing in the sample. Write words and sentences from the narrative on the lines below the keys.
4. At the bottom of the page, write one or two ideas for how the narrative could be stronger.

Introductory Paragraph

_____

_____

Body Paragraph

_____

_____

Body Paragraph

_____

_____

Body Paragraph

_____

_____

Conclusion

_____

_____

Final Evaluation

➤ Objective

Students will reread the second and final drafts of their narrative essays. They will also review and compare the scores they gave their writing on self-evaluations as well as scores they received from the teacher to answer reflective questions.

➤ Introduction

You will look back at the scores you gave your second draft on a self-evaluation. Then you will see the scores I gave the final draft of your narrative essay. You will compare the scores. Then you will answer questions about what you have learned about narrative writing.

➤ Instruction

Before today, you used rubrics to look closely at your writing. Rubrics can show us how our writing has improved over time. In the last module, you learned how to write a narrative paragraph. In this module, you wrote a longer narrative piece. Narrative writing has certain qualities. A narrator tells the story, or what happened in the experience. The experience happens in a certain place, called the setting. A narrative describes events that happen in an order that makes sense. Concrete words and details help describe the experience. The last paragraph ends the narrative. It may describe the effect the experience had on the author and readers. Today you will compare scores from different drafts of your narrative. This will help you see areas in which you have strengthened your writing.

➤ Guided Practice

Distribute students' copies of their second drafts and final drafts, along with their copies of "Self-Evaluation: Narrative Essay" (page 148) and "Teacher Evaluation: Narrative Essay" (page 153). Distribute "My Writing Progress" (page 154). *Reread the second draft of your narrative. Look at the scores you gave your writing on "Self-Evaluation: Narrative Essay." Find the chart on "My Writing Progress." First you will look at the boxes on the left side of the chart. Color the box that matches the score you gave your writing for each quality of narrative writing. Then reread the final draft of your narrative. Look at the scores you received on "Teacher Evaluation: Narrative Essay." Now you will use the boxes on the right side of the chart. Color the boxes that match the scores you received for each quality of narrative writing.*

➤ Independent Practice

Look at the scores on both sides of the chart on page 154. How do they compare? Use the colored chart to answer the questions in Part Two.

➤ Review

Review specific categories of the rubric, as needed, to help students match their scores with qualities of narrative writing to complete the chart on "My Writing Progress." Review the scores students received on the "Teacher Evaluation: Narrative Essay" to answer questions and clarify, as needed. Discuss with students possible reasons for differences in scores (student learning, editing, revising, areas in which they are still learning and developing their skills).

➤ Closing

You reread drafts of your narrative that you wrote at different times. You looked at scores you gave your writing and scores you received from me. Then you compared the scores to think about what you have learned about narrative writing.

Teacher Evaluation: Narrative Essay

Student Name: _____   Score: _____

	4	3	2	1
Narrator and/or Characters	The narrative introduces a narrator and/or characters who had an interesting family experience.	The narrative introduces a narrator and/or characters who had a family experience.	The narrative introduces a character who narrates an experience.	The narrative does not introduce the narrator or any characters.
Setting and Situation	The narrative introduces a setting and situation about an interesting family experience to orient readers.	The narrative introduces a situation about a family experience.	The narrative introduces a setting, but the situation is unclear.	The narrative does not introduce a setting or a situation.
Organization	The narrator describes events in an interesting family experience in an order that makes sense.	The narrator describes events in a family experience.	The narrator describes events in a family experience, but they are not in an order that makes sense.	The narrative does not describe events.
Dialogue and/or Description	The author uses dialogue and description to describe an interesting family experience and to show how characters respond.	The author uses dialogue and description to describe a family experience.	The author uses dialogue or description to describe an experience.	The author does not use dialogue or description well to describe an experience.
Details	The author includes concrete words and sensory details to describe events in the narrative about an interesting family experience.	The author includes concrete words or sensory details to describe events in the narrative about a family experience.	The author includes details to describe events in the narrative about an experience.	The author does not include specific details to describe events in the narrative.
Transition Words	The author uses transition words to guide readers through the sequence of events.	The author uses transition words in some places to show the order of events.	The author uses transition words once or twice to show the order of events.	The author does not use transition words to show the order of events.
Conclusion	The narrative has a conclusion that flows naturally from the narrated experience and provides a sense of closure.	The narrative has a conclusion that describes the end of the experience.	The narrative has a conclusion.	The narrative does not have a satisfactory conclusion.
Conventions	The narrative has correct writing conventions.	The narrative has a few errors in writing conventions, but they do not affect the meaning.	The narrative has writing convention errors that need editing for understanding.	The narrative has many writing convention errors that change the author's meaning.

Name(s): _____

My Writing Progress

➤ Part One

1. Look at the scores you gave your writing on "Self-Evaluation: Narrative Essay" (page 148). On the left side, color the box that matches the score you gave your writing for each quality of narrative writing.

2. Look at the scores you received on "Teacher Evaluation: Narrative Essay" (page 153). On the right side, color the box that matches the score you received for each quality of narrative writing.

4	3	2	1		1	2	3	4
				Introduce narrator and/or characters				
				Introduce setting and situation				
				Organized events				
				Dialogue and description				
				Details				
				Transition words				
				Conclusion				
				Conventions				
Self-Evaluation					**Teacher Evaluation**			

➤ Part Two

Look at the scores on each side of the chart and answer the questions.

1. What do you notice about the difference in the scores? _____

_____

2. In which areas did your scores improve? Why do you think this happened?

_____

_____

3. How are the scores different? _____

_____

4. In which areas did your scores stay the same? _____

_____

5. What is one thing you learned by comparing your scores in this way?

_____

_____

Writing Topics

➤ Opinion/Argumentative Writing

Module 1: Interesting Healthy Food

- The most interesting healthy food you have tasted
- Your favorite healthy food
- Why people should eat healthy foods
- Which healthy foods are good for kids to eat
- Healthy foods that kids like
- An interesting healthy food you would like to try

Module 2: School Clothes

- School uniforms
- Kids' choices in what they wear to school
- What kids should wear to school
- The best kind of school clothes
- School rules about what kids can wear to school
- Who decides what kids should wear to school

➤ Informative/Explanatory Writing

Module 3: Weather

- The most unusual weather you have seen
- Explain snow (or other weather) to someone who has not seen it
- How weather affects people
- An experience you have had in (extreme) weather
- Something you have learned about weather

Module 4: How Money Changes Over Time

- How colors have changed on money
- Which faces have changed on money
- Why our money changes
- The history of money design in our country
- Interesting features of money
- How coins have changed over time

Writing Topics *(cont.)*

➤ Narrative Writing

Module 5: Observing an Animal in Nature

- Animals you have seen on vacation
- Animals you have seen while visiting family or friends
- Animals you have seen in your community or neighborhood
- Animals you have seen while traveling
- Animals observed on a safari
- An experience you have had with an animal that is not a pet

Module 6: Interesting Family Stories

- An interesting family vacation or trip
- An interesting family experience for a special occasion
- An interesting family experience at home
- An interesting family experience with a particular family member
- An interesting or unique activity your family does together

Meeting Standards

Each passage and activity meets one or more of the following Common Core State Standards © Copyright 2010. National Governors Association Center for Best Practices and Council of Chief State School Officers. All rights reserved. For more information about the Common Core State Standards, go to http://www.corestandards.org/ or http://www.teachercreated.com/standards/.

Reading: Literature	Activities
Key Ideas and Details	
RL.2.1: Ask and answer such questions as *who, what, where, when, why,* and *how* to demonstrate understanding of key details in a text.	Visiting Relatives and Wildlife (M5) Review a Narrative (M5) A Great Family Experience (M6) The Keys to a Great Experience (M6)
Craft and Structure	
RL.2.4: Describe how words and phrases (e.g., regular beats, alliteration, rhymes, repeated lines) supply rhythm and meaning in a story, poem, or song.	Transition Words (M5) Review a Narrative (M5)
RL.2.5: Describe the overall structure of a story, including describing how the beginning introduces the story and the ending concludes the action.	Visiting Relatives and Wildlife (M5) Review a Narrative (M5) A Great Family Experience (M6) The Keys to a Great Experience (M6)

Reading: Informational Text	Activities
Key Ideas and Details	
RI.2.1: Ask and answer such questions as *who, what, where, when, why,* and *how* to demonstrate understanding of key details in a text.	Reasons for My Opinion (M1) Delightful Dip (M1) Review (M2) Weather Information (M3) Learning About the Weather (M3) Putting the Parts Together (M3) Facts and Details (M4) Rate a Sample Essay (M4)
RI.2.3: Describe the connection between a series of historical events, scientific ideas or concepts, or steps in technical procedures in a text.	Learning About the Weather (M3) Facts and Details (M4)
Craft and Structure	
RI.2.4: Determine the meaning of words and phrases in a text relevant to a *grade 2 topic or subject area.*	Mysterious Fog (M3) Clouds in the Sky (M3) Raindrops (M3) Learning About the Weather (M3) Snow Day (M3) Facts and Details (M4) Rate a Sample Essay (M4)
RI.2.6: Identify the main purpose of a text, including what the author wants to answer, explain, or describe.	Study an Opinion Paragraph (M1) My Opinion Counts (M1) What Is a Thesis Statement? (M2) Review (M2) Weather Information (M3) The Best Topic Sentences (M3) Bursting with Information (M3) Putting the Parts Together (M3) Rate a Sample Essay (M4)
Integration of Knowledge and Ideas	
RI.2.8: Describe how reasons support specific points the author makes in a text.	Study an Opinion Paragraph (M1) Reasons for My Opinion (M1) My Opinion Counts (M1) Review (M2)

Writing	Activities
Text Types and Purposes	
W.2.1: Write opinion pieces in which they introduce the topic or book they are writing about, state an opinion, supply reasons that support the opinion, use linking words (e.g., *because, and, also*) to connect opinion and reasons, and provide a concluding sentence or section.	Study an Opinion Paragraph (M1) Writing a Topic Sentence (M1) Reasons for My Opinion (M1) Connecting Reasons to an Opinion (M1) Different Opinions (M1) Delightful Dip (M1) Read and Respond (M1)

Meeting Standards *(cont.)*

Writing *(cont.)*	Activities
Text Types and Purposes *(cont.)*	
W.2.1: Write opinion pieces in which they introduce the topic or book they are writing about, state an opinion, supply reasons that support the opinion, use linking words (e.g., *because, and, also*) to connect opinion and reasons, and provide a concluding sentence or section. *(cont.)*	Second Draft and Self-Evaluation (M1) What I Notice About My Writing (M1) Final Draft (M1) Revising My Opinion Paragraph (M1) My Opinion Counts (M1) Planning My Essay (M2) Describing My Topic (M2) Explaining My Opinion (M2) Our Opinions Matter (M2) How to Write a Concluding Paragraph (M2) First Draft and Peer Review (M2) Second Draft and Self-Evaluation (M2)
W.2.2: Write informative/explanatory texts in which they introduce a topic, use facts and definitions to develop points, and provide a concluding statement or section.	Writing Topic Sentences (M3) Planning Ahead (M3) Learning About the Weather (M3) Supporting My Ideas (M3) Making Sense Out of Information (M3) Bursting with Information (M3) First Draft and Peer Review (M3) Second Draft and Self-Evaluation (M3) Final Draft (M3) Write an Introductory Paragraph (M4) Describing the Topic (M4) An Organized Essay (M4) Facts and Details (M4) My Conclusions from the Facts (M4) My Concluding Paragraph (M4) First Draft and Peer Review (M4) Second Draft and Self-Evaluation (M4)
W.2.3: Write narratives in which they recount a well-elaborated event or short sequence of events, include details to describe actions, thoughts, and feelings, use temporal words to signal event order, and provide a sense of closure.	Introduce Your Narrative (M5) Thinking About Narratives (M5) The Narrative Experience (M5) The Whole Experience (M5) The Perfect Word (M5) A Path Through the Narrative (M5) Strong Concluding Sentences (M5) First Draft and Peer Review (M5) Second Draft and Self-Evaluation (M5) Final Draft (M5) Clues to My Narrative (M6) Picture My Narrative (M6) What People Say (M6) Describing the Experience (M6) Action Steps (M6) A Great Family Experience (M6) The Final Event (M6) First Draft and Peer Review (M6) Second Draft and Self-Evaluation (M6)
Production and Distribution of Writing	
W.2.5: With guidance and support from adults and peers, focus on a topic and strengthen writing as needed by revising and editing.	Reasons for My Opinion (M1) Connecting Reasons to an Opinion (M1) Read and Respond (M1) What I Notice About My Writing (M1) Revising My Opinion Paragraph (M1) Learning from Differences (M1) Learning About a Topic (M2) Our Opinions Matter (M2) How to Write a Concluding Paragraph (M2) Opinion Essay Checklist (M2) Second Draft and Self-Evaluation (M2) Supporting My Ideas (M3) Bursting with Information (M3)

Meeting Standards *(cont.)*

Writing *(cont.)*	Activities
Production and Distribution of Writing *(cont.)*	
W.2.5: With guidance and support from adults and peers, focus on a topic and strengthen writing as needed by revising and editing. *(cont.)*	Helping Each Other (M3) What's the Difference? (M3) Trading Information (M4) My Conclusions from the Facts (M4) My Concluding Paragraph (M4) First Draft and Peer Review (M4) Final Evaluation (M4) Thinking About Narratives (M5) The Whole Experience (M5) The Perfect Word (M5) Strong Concluding Sentences (M5) Peer Review (M5) Second Draft and Self-Evaluation (M5) Final Draft (M5) Final Evaluation (M5) Clues to My Narrative (M6) What People Say (M6) Describing the Experience (M6) First Draft and Peer Review (M6) Helping Each Other Write (M6) Second Draft and Self-Evaluation (M6)
W.2.6: With guidance and support from adults, use a variety of digital tools to produce and publish writing, including in collaboration with peers.	Final Draft (M3) Concluding Paragraphs (M4) Final Draft (M5)
Research to Build and Present Knowledge	
W.2.7: Participate in shared research and writing projects (e.g., read a number of books on a single topic to produce a report; record science observations).	Planning Ahead (M3) Learning About the Weather (M3) Facts and Details (M4) My Conclusions from the Facts (M4)
W.2.8: Recall information from experiences or gather information from provided sources to answer a question.	Planning Ahead (M3) Learning About the Weather (M3) Facts and Details (M4) What People Say (M6) Action Steps (M6) My Writing Progress (M6)

Speaking & Listening	Activities
Comprehension and Collaboration	
SL.2.1: Participate in collaborative conversations with diverse partners about *grade 2 topics and texts* with peers and adults in small and larger groups.	*all*
SL.2.2: Recount or describe key ideas or details from a text read aloud or information presented orally or through other media.	Interesting Narratives (M5) Strong Concluding Sentences (M5) Review (M5) Picture My Narrative (M6) Helping Each Other Write (M6)
SL.2.3: Ask and answer questions about what a speaker says in order to clarify comprehension, gather additional information, or deepen understanding of a topic or issue.	Topic Sentences (M1) Learning About a Topic (M2) Our Opinions Matter (M2) Supporting My Ideas (M3) Concluding Sentences (M3) Bursting with Information (M3) Strong Concluding Sentences (M5) Clues to My Narrative (M6) Picture My Narrative (M6) Helping Each Other Write (M6)

Meeting Standards (cont.)

Speaking & Listening (cont.)	Activities
Presentation of Knowledge and Ideas	
SL.2.4: Tell a story or recount an experience with appropriate facts and relevant, descriptive details, speaking audibly in coherent sentences.	Picture My Narrative (M6) Helping Each Other Write (M6)
SL.2.6: Produce complete sentences when appropriate to task and situation in order to provide requested detail or clarification.	*all*

Language	Activities
Conventions of Standard English	
L.2.1: Demonstrate command of the conventions of standard English grammar and usage when writing or speaking.	*all*
L.2.2: Demonstrate command of the conventions of standard English capitalization, punctuation, and spelling when writing.	*all*
Knowledge of Language	
L.2.3: Use knowledge of language and its conventions when writing, speaking, reading, or listening.	*all*
Vocabulary Acquisition and Use	
L.2.4: Determine or clarify the meaning of unknown and multiple-meaning words and phrases based on grade 2 reading and content, choosing flexibly from an array of strategies.	Descriptive Words (M1) Describing My Topic (M2) Mysterious Fog (M3) When the Wind Blows (M3) Clouds in the Sky (M3) Weather Words (M3) Facts and Details (M4) The Perfect Word (M5) Action Steps (M6)
L.2.5: Demonstrate understanding of word relationships and nuances in word meanings.	Study an Opinion Paragraph (M1) Descriptive Words (M1) Read and Respond (M1) Describing My Topic (M2) Weather Words (M3) Describing the Topic (M4) An Organized Essay (M4) Introduce Your Narrative (M5) The Whole Experience (M5) Peer Review (M5) Describing the Experience (M6)
L.2.6: Use words and phrases acquired through conversations, reading and being read to, and responding to texts, including using adjectives and adverbs to describe (e.g., *When other kids are happy that makes me happy*).	Descriptive Words (M1) Reasons for My Opinion (M1) Connecting Reasons to an Opinion (M1) Describing My Topic (M2) Explaining My Opinion (M2) Weather Words (M3) Supporting My Ideas (M3) Trading Information (M4) Describing the Topic (M4) An Organized Essay (M4) Facts and Details (M4) Final Evaluation (M4) Introduce Your Narrative (M5) The Narrative Experience (M5) The Whole Experience (M5) The Perfect Word (M5) A Path Through the Narrative (M5) What People Say (M6) Describing the Experience (M6)